Evidence-based Child Forensic Interviewing

Evidence-based Child Forensic Interviewing

THE DEVELOPMENTAL NARRATIVE ELABORATION INTERVIEW

Interviewer Guide

Karen J. Saywitz • Lorinda B. Camparo

OXFORD

UNIVERSITY PRESS

OXFORD
UNIVERSITY PRESS

Oxford University press is a department of the University of Oxford.
It furthers the University's objective of excellence in research, scholarship,
and education by publishing worldwide.

Oxford   New York
Auckland   Cape Town   Dar es Salaam   Hong Kong   Karachi
Kuala Lumpur   Madrid   Melbourne   Mexico City   Nairobi
New Delhi   Shanghai   Taipei   Toronto

With offices in
Argentina   Austria   Brazil   Chile   Czech Republic   France   Greece
Guatemala   Hungary   Italy   Japan   Poland   Portugal   Singapore
South Korea   Switzerland   Thailand   Turkey   Ukraine   Vietnam

Oxford is a registered trademark of Oxford University Press in the UK
and certain other countries.

Published in the United States of America by
Oxford University Press
198 Madison Avenue, New York, NY 10016

Library of Congress Cataloging-in-Publication Data
Saywitz, Karen Jill.
Evidence-based child forensic interviewing : the developmental narrative
elaboration interview / Karen J. Saywitz, Lorinda B. Camparo.
    pages cm
Includes bibliographical references.
ISBN 978–0–19–973089–6
1. Interviewing in law enforcement.   2. Child witnesses.   I. Camparo, Lorinda B.   II. Title.
HV8073.3.S29 2014
363.25'4083—dc23
2013022450

9 8 7 6 5 4 3 2 1
Printed in the United States of America
on acid-free paper

About Programs *ThatWork*™

Stunning developments in health care have taken place over the last several years, but many of our widely accepted interventions and strategies in mental health and behavioral medicine have been brought into question by research evidence as not only lacking benefit, but perhaps, even inducing harm. Other strategies have been proven effective using the best current standards of evidence, resulting in broad-based recommendations to make these practices more available to the public.

Several recent developments are behind this revolution. First, we have arrived at a much deeper understanding of pathology, both psychological and physical, which has led to the development of new, more precisely targeted interventions. Second, our research methodologies have improved substantially, such that we have reduced threats to internal and external validity, making the outcomes more directly applicable to clinical situations. Third, governments around the world and health care systems and policymakers have decided that the quality of care should improve, that it should be evidence-based, and that it is in the public's interest to ensure that this happens (Barlow, 2004; Institute of Medicine, 2001).

Of course, the major stumbling block for clinicians everywhere is the accessibility of newly developed evidence-based psychological interventions. Workshops and books can go only so far in acquainting responsible and conscientious practitioners with the latest behavioral health care practices and their applicability to individual patients. This new series, Programs *ThatWork*™, is devoted to communicating these exciting new interventions to clinicians on the front lines of practice.

The manuals and workbooks in this series contain step-by-step detailed procedures for assessing and treating specific problems and diagnoses.

But this series also goes beyond the books and manuals by providing ancillary materials that will approximate the supervisory process in assisting practitioners in the implementation of these procedures in their practice.

In our emerging health care system, the growing consensus is that following evidence-based practice procedures is the most responsible course of action for the mental health professional. All behavioral health care clinicians deeply desire to provide the best possible care for their patients. In this series, our aim is to close the dissemination and information gap and make that possible.

This guide addresses the discrepancy between the requirements of forensic interviews and the abilities of young children to perform well when faced with this situation. Young children are frequently called upon to communicate needed forensic information, but this requires myriad developmental skills they have not yet mastered. Their brains are still developing abilities in language, comprehension, memory recall, resistance to suggestion, and emotional maturity, and without accommodations to their individual level of development, interviews can produce false reports, stress, frustration (for child and interviewer), and miscommunication.

The Developmental Narrative Elaboration (DNE) Interview, created by Drs. Karen J. Saywitz and Lorinda B. Camparo and outlined in this guide, offers an evidence-based interview template and set of techniques for professionals in mental health, social service, law enforcement, and law, designed to help children ages four to 12 reliably tell as much as they can about their experiences and perceptions. This semi-structured process respects legal requirements as well as social science; it is based on child development research, child forensic interviewing research, and Saywitz and Camparo's own tested strategies for improving children's recall and communication of forensically relevant information. Divided into three main phases, the DNE helps the interviewer guide children to understand the unfamiliar context, teaches the Narrative Elaboration Strategy, and provides unbiased recall cues and tips to help enhance the child's memory and reduce potential miscommunication and suggestibility.

This empirically supported guide is a much-needed resource that will be invaluable to professionals who conduct forensic interviews with children and want to get the most accurate information while minimizing children's stress, accommodating their developmental limitations, and maximizing their strengths and abilities.

David H. Barlow, Editor-in-Chief
Programs ThatWork™
Boston, Massachusetts

References

Barlow, D. H. (2004). Psychological treatments. *American Psychologist, 59,* 869–878.

Institute of Medicine. (2001). *Crossing the Quality Chasm: A New Health System for the Twenty-first Century.* Washington, DC: National Academy Press.

Contents

Appendices

Acknowledgments

The authors would like to thank their many colleagues who have contributed to the development of the Developmental Narrative Elaboration Interview. We especially want to thank our research collaborators: Lynn Snyder, Rebecca Nathanson, Joyce Dorado, Susan Moan-Hardie, Vivian Lamphear, and Carol Jaenicke. We would like thank Deirdre Brown and Carole Peterson for their research on narrative elaboration and for their comments on a draft of this book. Appreciation is also extended to our mentors, Shari Diamond and Milton Miller, without whom this work would not have been possible, and our families, Richard, Sarah, Anna, James, Robyn, and Stayce.

Evidence-based Child Forensic Interviewing

Chapter 1   *Introductory Information for Interviewers*

Background Information and Purpose of This Program

This book describes the Developmental Narrative Elaboration (DNE) interview. The DNE is a step-by-step process for interviewing children in a forensic context that respects both legal requirements and social science research. It is an evidence-based approach derived from three sources of data: (a) the long-standing research literature on child development; (b) contemporary research on child interviewing; and (c) studies of our own innovative strategies for improving children's recall and communication of forensically relevant information. The DNE is comprised of a core template for interviewing children as well as a set of individual evidence-based techniques that can be embedded into the core template at the interviewer's discretion as cases unfold. In addition, the DNE incorporates best-practice principles derived from an emerging consensus among professional organizations in the field. (See Saywitz & Camparo, 2009; and Saywitz, Lyon, & Goodman, 2011, for further discussion.)

The DNE interview is designed to elicit reliable information from children in a wide array of contexts where the results of the interview will serve as input for legal and social-service decision making. Settings run the gamut, from social workers and police officers in the field making decisions about child protection and adult culpability; to private-practice clinicians in their offices evaluating suspicions of child maltreatment; to attorneys involved in dependency, family, civil, or criminal court cases. The DNE is a cross-disciplinary approach intended to serve the needs of professionals in mental health, social service, law enforcement, and the legal system.

The DNE was designed to address a problem all interviewers face—an inherent mismatch between the demands of the forensic context and the capabilities of young children. Forensic interviews differ from traditional clinical interviews and from everyday conversation (see Saywitz, Esplin, & Romanoff, 2007, for further discussion). They require a host of abilities and skills that children may not yet have mastered, as these skills develop gradually as children's brains mature and they gain experience in the world around them. At a minimum, the forensic interview demands that children translate their memories and perceptions into verbal responses within a question-and-answer format, often in an unfamiliar setting. Frequently, high levels of attention, language production, comprehension, knowledge, reasoning, memory retrieval, resistance to suggestion, perspective-taking, and emotional maturity are required. Without accommodations to the child's developmental level, the demands of the forensic interview can outstrip a child's abilities, leading to miscommunication, misinterpretation, false reports, and unnecessary stress on both children and interviewers.

To close the gap, the DNE provides the scaffolding, structure, and guidance children often need to perform optimally; that is, at a more advanced level than their developmental limitations normally allow.[1] This is accomplished by a template that lowers task demands to a child's developmental level and by a set of evidence-based memory and communication strategies that improve children's performance. The DNE furnishes children with the knowledge necessary to understand the unfamiliar forensic context and task demands, provides unbiased retrieval cues to help children organize their memory search, and utilizes optional instructions and preparation to enhance memory and reduce potential for miscommunication and suggestibility.

What Is the Developmental Narrative Elaboration Interview?

The DNE is a semi-structured interview procedure designed for children four to 12 years of age.[2] The goal is to help children to tell as much as they can about their experiences and perceptions to the best of their ability and in their own words, without tainting their reports. It consists of three principal phases.

Phase I

Phase I is a preliminary phase that includes introductions, rapport development, and explanations to increase children's awareness of how the forensic interview differs from everyday conversation, plus optional strategies for enhancing memory reports, improving comprehension of follow-up questions, and reducing suggestion.

Phase II

Phase II involves eliciting children's statements; we refer to this stage as the Core Interview. It comprises three steps: Free Recall, Cued Elaboration, and Short Answer Follow-up Questions. Each step lays a foundation for the step that follows and builds on the step that precedes it.

Free Recall

In the first step, interviewers create an opportunity for children to give a spontaneous or minimally prompted narrative of a potentially forensically relevant incident(s) (e.g., "What happened?"), followed by one or two simple, open-ended prompts (e.g., "Tell me more" or "What happened next?").

Cued Elaboration

In the second step, interviewers provide a unique opportunity for further elaboration by helping children structure their memory search with generic, non-suggestive verbal or visual cues. (The visual cues are simple line drawings that can be photocopied from Appendices A and B and cut into individual cards.) These verbal and visual cues prompt children to provide additional detail in their own words about four empirically-derived categories of information: (a) participants, (b) locations, (c) actions, and (d) the conversations and affective states of participants. This process provides interviewers with a larger data set of information from which to craft better-informed, and potentially less-biased, follow-up questions for the third step.

Short Answer Follow-up Questions

In the third step, interviewers employ specific follow-up questions to double back and explore any important, vague, and inconsistent information mentioned by the child in order to elicit further elaboration, clarification, and explanation. These questions are formulated according to evidence-based guidelines for generating developmentally appropriate and non-leading questions.

Phase III

Finally, Phase III is a time for closure. It consists of guidelines for closing the interview to address children's questions and educate them about next steps, to help children regain their composure if upset, and to identify potential stressors and generate anticipatory coping strategies. Table 1.1 provides an overview of the interview process. Each phase is presented in detail in the remaining chapters of this book.

Table 1.1 Overview Checklist of DNE Interview

Phase I: Preliminary Phase

- **Setting**: Create a physical and psycho-social setting to facilitate, not undermine, the child's motivation, cooperation, and effort.
  - Create a private, safe, child-friendly, warm, non-judgmental atmosphere.
  - Outline the mechanics of what will happen during the interview.
  - Use introductions to place the interview in context. Explain interview objectives, your role, and the child's role.
  - Demystify the legal process. Educate the child about the information-gathering and decision-making process in a developmentally appropriate fashion.
- **Rapport**: Take time to develop rapport and create a conversational template for the interview to follow.
  - Consider suggested activities for breaking the ice and developing rapport.

continued

Table 1.1 Overview Checklist of DNE Interview *continued*

- Using open-ended questions that require multi-word responses, model a style of discourse that demonstrates the child is expected to tell as much as possible in his own words, with minimal prompting.

- If met with ambivalence, silence, or reluctance, consider suggested activities for understanding and working around a child's reasons for reticence.

- **Optional Strategies**: Teach optional strategies for improving memory and communication.

  - Teach narrative elaboration strategy with reminder cards. (*optional*)

  - Teach strategies for improving communication. (*optional*)

  - Teach strategies for resisting suggestive questions. (*optional*)

- **Interview Pointers**: Provide pointers as deemed necessary from toolkit of options.

  - Select from a list of explanations designed to increase children's awareness of how the forensic interview differs from everyday conversation.

Phase II: Eliciting Children's Statements with the Core Interview

- **Step One—Free Recall:** Provide an opportunity for minimally prompted or spontaneous descriptions of a forensically relevant event(s). Follow with simple open-ended prompts for elaboration.

- **Step Two—Cued Elaboration:** Provide an additional opportunity for elaboration on the Participants, Setting, Actions, Conversation, and Affective States with either visual or verbal DNE category cues.

- **Step Three—Follow-up Questions:**

  - Use short-answer questions that require multi-word responses to return to important information for further elaboration, clarification, and explanation.

  - When questions requiring one-word answers are necessary, follow up with requests to elaborate or explain so you are certain a child's response means what you think it means.

  - Follow guidelines to formulate non-leading and developmentally sensitive questions.

- Continuously evaluate when to proceed and when to terminate.

- Consider the merits of introducing the topic of interest by referring to verifiable information from outside sources.

Phase III: Closure

- Take time for closure. Review key points. Give children a chance to ask questions.

- Educate the child about next steps and dispel fears when possible.

- Identify anticipated problems and plan positive strategies for coping as needed.

- Check for safety issues and make referrals as needed.

How Does the DNE Address the Interviewer's Dilemma?

In the sections that follow, we highlight immaturities that the DNE is designed to address in children's memory, communicative competence, resistance to suggestion, cognition, and social skills.

Addressing Limitations on Children's Memory Reports

Children are able to recall a remarkable amount of information about past autobiographical events, especially highly salient, unique, emotionally engaging, and meaningful events (Bauer, 2007; Nelson & Fivush, 2004), and these are exactly the types of events most likely to be relevant in the forensic context. However, the completeness and accuracy of young children's recall is highly dependent on the way children are questioned (Larsson & Lamb, 2009). The information children report in response to *free recall* tasks where they generate the answer from their own memory (e.g., responses to "What happened?") is generally accurate but incomplete. Often, information is elicited piecemeal by adult questions that drive the organization of the material and guide the memory search.

It would not be uncommon for a five-year-old who is asked, "What did you do after school today?" to respond with "We played." Further details would require additional questions from the adult, for example:

Adult: "Who did you play with?"

Child: "Mary and Bob";

Adult: "What did you do?"

Child: "Play on the swings";

Adult: "Where did you do that?"

Child: "At the playground";

Adult: "Which playground?"

Child: "The one in the park."

Hence, young children's spontaneous and independent free recall of past events (e.g., "We played") is often skeletal and insufficient for forensic decision-making. It is difficult to elicit sufficient information without additional questions; however, if questions are misleading, they can distort children's reports. Children's responses to specific follow-up questions, such as true-or-false or multiple-choice questions where children need only verify if they recognize the information in the question, can provide sought-after additional detail, but these responses are not nearly as accurate as free recall or answers to open-ended questions (e.g., Lamb et al., 2003; Waterman, Blades, & Spencer, 2001).

Eventually, children develop self-cueing strategies as they learn which questions to ask themselves in order to include the *who*, *what*, *when*, and *where* in their narratives independently. However, prior to attaining this mastery, they have limited perspective-taking skills and may not understand what information is important or expected by the interviewer. Similarly, their metamemory skills are immature, so their awareness of how their own memory works is limited and faulty. Also, young children often reason from an egocentric viewpoint (Piaget, 1926), have difficulty drawing inferences about the listener's perspective, and possess limited referential communication skills, all of which can contribute to their failure to orient the listener fully to person, place, context, and timing (Flavell, Botkin, Fry, Wright, & Jarvis, 1968; Robinson & Robinson, 1978). Compounding the problem, young children have not mastered the grammar required to add the prepositional phrases, adverbs, adjectives, and embedded clauses that typically provide the type of detail needed in forensic investigations. When all of these skills are mastered, they can finally provide detailed relevant information independently in a response to a general open-ended prompt like "What happened?" However, all of these skills are continuing to develop between first and third grade. Until then, young children benefit from all the non-leading help they can get from the way the interview is conducted.

As you can see from the preceding example, children's narratives begin as fairly skeletal descriptions; loosely organized, idiosyncratic, and dependent on context to facilitate retrieval (e.g., Nelson, 1986; Peterson, 1990). Their narrative ability is impeded by their limited event knowledge (understanding the causal and temporal relations among events) and by their impoverished scripts for events to guide attention, retrieval, and retention processes. Studies of children's event knowledge (e.g., generalized scripts for common events) suggest that event recall is guided by psychologically salient constructs that include the categories of *participants, setting, actions, consequences, conversations, and affective states* (Mandler & Johnson, 1977; Stein & Glenn, 1978). There is an extensive literature on children's story-recall that demonstrates that they naturally use these categories to organize information.

In addition to their limited narrative skills, young children have more difficulty actually retrieving information from memory than do older children and adults, who use more complex and successful retrieval strategies to increase the amount of information they retrieve independently (Ornstein, Naus, & Liberty, 1975; Pressley & Levin, 1977; Schneider & Pressley, 1989). Preschoolers show rudimentary use of retrieval strategies on simple tasks; hence, three-year-olds require a great deal of prompting, whereas five-year-olds require less. From four to 12 years of age, children demonstrate increasing efficiency and flexibility in retrieval-strategy usage (Kobasigawa, 1977). Complex heuristics resulting in exhaustive memory searches are rarely seen until the end of grade school and may not be mastered until adolescence (Salatas & Flavell, 1976). However, experimental studies clearly demonstrate that young children can benefit from learning new memory strategies they could not have generated on their own, and they can deploy these strategies to improve memory reports with adult guidance during the memory test (Schneider & Pressley, 1989). Young children perform best when they are able to benefit from supportive strategies, including cueing (Elischberger & Roebers, 2001; Geddie, Beer, Bartosik, & Wuensch, 2001; Pipe, Lamb, Orbach, & Esplin, 2004).

Hence, the DNE is designed to take full advantage of children's memory strengths and compensate for their memory weaknesses; that is, to take advantage of the fact that children's initial free-recall narratives are most accurate (e.g., Adult: "What happened?" Child: "We played"), and to compensate for their difficulty in retrieving details and narrating past events independently. Our approach relies on the fact that children can organize and recall stories and events in terms of categories of information mentioned above (e.g., participants, setting, actions, consequences, and conversations/affective states), and they can learn to use new memory strategies with adult guidance and prompting to improve recall. With the DNE,

(a)   the interviewer helps the child provide more fully elaborated
         narratives in response to simple event-category cues that structure

recall efforts without the use of specific or potentially leading questions.

(b) This interim step of cued-elaboration provides a larger base of more accurate detail in response to open-ended prompts on which to base specific follow-up questions.

(c) Interviewers have the option, during the preliminary phase, of teaching children to use visual category-cues to organize elaboration or the option of using verbal category-cues during the core interview without any preliminary teaching activities.

In addition, the DNE includes instructions to children to be as complete in their answers as they can on their own, including details they might not think are very important, thereby allowing the adult to be the ultimate judge of the forensic relevance of the details (Saywitz, Geiselman, & Bornstein, 1992). However, the DNE does not encourage children to provide details at any cost, as there can be a trade-off between quantity and accuracy, especially for young children three to five years of age (Kulkofsky, Wang, & Ceci, 2008). Instead, interviewers can model the level of detail expected and practice with corrective feedback. Also, interviewers use initial conversation during the preliminary phase to demonstrate that children are expected to tell as much as possible in their own words with minimal prompting in response to open-ended questions. Interviewers instruct children to tell the truth, to tell only what they really remember, and not to guess or make anything up, as recent studies have underscored the utility of instructing children to tell the truth to enhance the accuracy of their reports (Lyon, Malloy, Quas, & Talwar, 2008).

Addressing Limitations on Children's Communicative Competence

In addition to growth in memory ability, studies are clear that children develop the ability to produce and comprehend language gradually (Owens, 2011). Field studies show that child witnesses are often asked questions that are phrased in grammar too complex and vocabulary too sophisticated for young children to comprehend (e.g., Brennan & Brennan, 1988; Evans, Lee, & Lyon, 2009; Perry et al., 1995). The majority of communication breakdowns occur with children in the three- to eight-year-old range, a period of rapid growth and development. Preschoolers' conversations are replete with irrelevant responses that can result from multiple sources. For example, mis-hearing, or mistaking unfamiliar words for familiar similar-sounding words, is common (e.g., assuming "jury" refers to "journey" or "jewelry"; "allegation" refers to "alligators"; "testify" is like "taking a test") (Saywitz, Jaenicke, & Camparo, 1990), in part because auditory-discrimination skills are not fully developed until around 10 to 11 years of age (Ingram, 1976). Additionally, children often assume the common definition for a term when the adult has an infrequent definition in mind; for example, assuming a "court" is a place to play basketball, a "minor" is someone who digs coal, a "date" is "something my mommy does with her boyfriend," or a "charge" is something one does with a credit card (Saywitz et al., 1990). Comprehension of adult grammar, vocabulary, and discourse rules continues to develop through eight to 10 years of age.

Compounding the problem when answering follow-up questions, young children have difficulty monitoring whether or not they fully understand adult language and often attempt to answer questions they do not understand, resulting in confusion and apparent inconsistency (e.g., Markman, 1981). For example, in one study, out of over 900 confusing, complex questions asked to 30 children, there were only nine instances in which children indicated non-comprehension (Carter, Bottoms, & Levine, 1996). Preschoolers even try to answer ambiguous, bizarre questions, such as "Is milk bigger than water?" (Hughes & Grieve, 1980). In one of our studies, six- to eight-year-olds were confronted with complex syntax and sophisticated vocabulary that exceeded their level of language comprehension (Saywitz, Snyder, & Nathanson, 1999). Most children tried to answer anyway, rarely asking for clarification and instead taking their turn in the conversation. Often, their answers were an association to a part of the question, usually the beginning (primacy effects) or the ending (recency effects), but not the answer to the intended question. This stands in sharp contrast to the high levels of accurate memory for the same events demonstrated when questions were phrased simply, using short utterances, simple grammar, and one- or two-syllable words. Metalinguistic awareness and comprehension-monitoring skills develop gradually, with many children entering elementary school demonstrating difficulties, and with continued improvements between seven and nine years of age (Saywitz & Wilkinson, 1982).

Based on findings in the field of communicative development, the DNE

(a)   offers guidelines for phrasing questions in simple grammar and vocabulary that young children are likely to comprehend, and

(b)   includes instructions and strategies to help children notice when they fail to comprehend; and once they identify instances of non-comprehension, to ask for rephrasing, rather than guess at an answer (Cordón, Saetermoe, & Goodman, 2005; Lamb & Brown, 2006; Peters & Nunez, 1999; Saywitz et al., 1999).

Addressing Children's Suggestibility

Another weakness of young children's reports is their vulnerability to misleading, suggestive, or option-posing questions from adults (e.g., yes or no, multiple choice). This is especially true of accusatory questions, tag questions (e.g., "He hurt you, *didn't he*?"), negative-term-insertion questions (e.g., "*Didn't* he hurt you?"), and suppositional questions where information is presumed without the opportunity to deny or confirm (e.g., "When he hurt you, were his clothes on or off?") (e.g., Bruck, Ceci, Francoeur, & Barr, 1995; Leichtman & Ceci, 1995; Lepore & Sesco, 1994).

In addition, many studies have shown that practice in answering open-ended questions unrelated to the target event, prior to the substantive interview, produces positive effects on amount of information reported in the field (Sternberg et al., 1997) and on accuracy of recall in the laboratory (e.g., Roberts, Lamb, & Sternberg, 2004; Saywitz et al., 1992; Saywitz & Snyder, 1996). Early practice answering open-ended questions, for example during rapport development, sets up expectations in the mind of the child regarding the type of discourse to follow (Pipe et al., 2004).

Another factor that contributes to children's heightened suggestibility is that they have a tendency to defer to adults as authority figures. In one memory study, preschoolers were more likely to go along with misleading suggestions when made by adult interviewers than when the same questions were asked by older children (Ceci, Ross, & Toglia, 1987). Yet when the adult stated he had no special knowledge of what happened, the suggestibility effects with preschoolers were mitigated (Toglia, Ross, Ceci, & Hembrooke, 1992). Similarly, studies using ethnographic-interview strategies emphasize the need to reduce the power differential between the child and the adult, ensuring the child understands that he or she is the expert on their own memories and perceptions.

Young children also tend to trust adult knowledge. Even three-year-olds understand that adults have a superior knowledge base (Taylor, Cartwright, & Bowden, 1991). Hence, a child might not recognize that adult interviewers do not know the answers to their own questions. In one study of second graders, children gave concrete answers stating they thought the interviewer already knew the answers to his questions because "He was looking at his paper where the answers were written down" (Saywitz & Nathanson, 1993a). During the preschool years, children are still in the process of acquiring a great deal of understanding about the way knowledge and beliefs are acquired (Flavell & Miller, 1998); for example, that some beliefs are true and some false, or that one can hold a belief with more or less certainty (e.g., Moore & Furrow, 1991). Hence, young children may not understand that suggestions embedded in leading questions are often unintentional attempts to elicit vital details, born out of frustration, rather than commands to say what the children believe interviewers want to hear. Children may not understand that in this unique context they are in a position to "correct" adult assumptions and preconceptions.

Based on the literature on children's suggestibility, the DNE is designed to minimize suggestibility by including

(a) a preparatory phase in which children practice answering open-ended questions;

(b) optional instructions informing children that the child, not the interviewer, is the expert on what happened at the event, because the interviewer was not present;

(c) optional instructions informing children that interviewers might put their guess into a question and that children should correct the interviewer when necessary, and (optional) practice recognizing such questions and correcting the interviewer;

(d) guidelines for interviewers on avoiding suggestive-question types when follow-up questions are necessary, relying instead on questions that require multi-word responses; and finally,

(e) an interim step of cued-elaboration as an additional opportunity for the child to elaborate on initial narratives prior to follow-up questions, thereby reducing the need for specific questions that are potentially leading.

Addressing Limitations on Children's Cognitive Abilities

Contemporary studies of infant brain activity show that we are born with amazingly sophisticated attentional abilities. In fact, younger children are often remarkably adept at noticing subtle, unexpected events (Gopnik, 2009). Unfortunately, this is in part due to the fact that children have less control over their attentional resources and less ability to inhibit distraction than adults do. Between the ages of four and six years, children develop greater resistance to both visual and auditory distractions (Holtz & Lehman, 1995). Yet children under the ages of five-to-seven are especially distracted by the "perceptual pull" of their physical surroundings—what they can see, hear, and touch in the "here and now"—hence the need to minimize visual and auditory distractions, and the potential value of providing visual cues that prompt recall and focus their attention on the task at hand. In addition, studies suggest young children benefit from repeated instructions to pay attention, and from redirection to the task at hand (Kannass, Colombo, & Wyss, 2010).

Additionally, forensic questions often demand information and academic skills that exceed young children's knowledge base. Frequently, questions require answers in terms of conventional units of measurement that are mastered gradually over the course of elementary school. Questions such as "How tall was he?" "How much did he weigh?" and "How old was he?" require describing someone's height, weight, or age in terms of feet, inches, pounds, or years. Questions such as "When did that happen?" "What time was it?" "What day was it?" or "What month was it?" require placing an event in time using the days of the week, months of the year, seasons of the year, calendar dates, hours of the day, or minutes of the hour (Wandrey, Lyon, Quas, & Friedman, 2011). However, many children do not even begin learning to tell time until first grade. The common question "How many times did that happen?" requires counting events in time, a more difficult task than counting physical objects, and can necessitate the use of addition and even multiplication. Questions such as "How far was it from your home?" "Where did he take you?" "What street did he go down?" and "What city?" require children to estimate distance in feet, inches, or miles as well as to use cognitive maps and employ geographical knowledge that the average five-year-old has yet to master. A developmentally sensitive approach avoids asking young children such questions until they have mastered the underlying skills.

Moreover, studies are clear that children under eight years of age often have difficulty drawing inferences and taking another's perspective or point of view (Dickson, 1981; Shantz, 1975). They have a limited understanding of causality and abstract hypothetical-deductive reasoning (see Bruner, 1957; Flavell, 1985; or Piaget, 1930). Children's metacognitive skills develop rapidly between seven and nine years of age (Flavell, 1981). Younger children can have difficulty analyzing and evaluating their own thoughts as independent "objects," and as a result, they often do not know what they do not know. The development of metacognition and inferential reasoning allows older children to infer the interviewer's (and possibly the alleged perpetrator's) intentions more accurately.

Also, younger children have difficulty reasoning about such abstract concepts as justice and society, and have limited and flawed knowledge of the legal or social service systems (Flin, Stevenson, & Davies, 1989; Saywitz, 1989; Warren-Leubecker, Tate, Hinton, & Ozbek, 1989). This can lead to incomplete reports and unrealistic fears (Sas, Austin, Wolfe, & Hurley, 1991; Saywitz, Nathanson, Snyder, & Lamphear, 1993, Experiment 7). Researchers have shown that young children can learn basic facts about the legal process when the information is presented at their developmental level, and in fact, that greater knowledge may be associated with less stress (lowered heart rate while answering questions) and greater recall (Nathanson & Saywitz, 2003).

In an effort to address some of the preceding limitations, the DNE seeks to accommodate children's cognitive immaturities by

(a) offering guidelines for creating a child-friendly atmosphere that minimizes visual and auditory distractions;

(b) instructing children to pay attention and listen carefully, and redirecting them to the task at hand;

(c) providing (optional) visual reminder cues that may help some children focus on the task at hand;

(d) making an effort to demystify the legal process and the interviewer's intentions by giving children clear, concrete explanations of the interview purpose, child and interviewer roles, and relevant aspects of the legal fact-finding and decision-making process in language and concepts they can understand; and

(e) providing guidelines for avoiding questions that require abstract concepts and reasoning skills that are likely to be beyond a child's phase of cognitive development.

Addressing Limitations on Children's Social Skills

Young children are accustomed to interacting with a limited number of familiar adults (e.g., parents, teachers, relatives). They often experience anxiety upon separation from familiar attachment figures. Furthermore, they have a limited repertoire of strategies for coping with the fear and anxiety they experience (Cramer, 1981). Studies show that supportive interviewers elicit more reliable reports than do intimidating ones. When social support is not tied to specific content, it helps young children (three- to seven-year-olds) be more resistant to misleading questions and improves the accuracy of their performance, without contaminating their accounts, even after a one-year delay (Bottoms, Quas, & Davis, 2007).

However, it is important to remember that research indicates supportiveness should not become selective reinforcement of responses that fit interviewers' *a priori* beliefs. In experimental studies where researchers manipulate the effects of *a priori* interviewer knowledge, biased interviewers tend to ask more leading questions in accordance with their preconceptions, clearly supporting the importance of interviewer objectivity (e.g., Bruck, Ceci, & Hembrooke, 1998; Quas et al., 2007).

Selective reinforcement of *a priori* beliefs can be especially dangerous when mixed with specific questions that are answered by "yes" or "no" (e.g., "Did Jack take the money?" "Did your mom hit you?"). In one study, children were given positive feedback for following the interviewer's lead (e.g., "Great!") and negative feedback when they failed to follow her lead ("You're not doing well."). When asked misleading questions, the group given positive feedback assented far more often than a group asked the same questions but given no feedback at all (Garven, Wood, & Malpass, 2000). When interviewers in research studies are given biased information about an event and left to formulate their own questions, they tend to ask yes–no questions for which the desired answer is "yes," in lieu of less-leading options (White, Leichtman, & Ceci, 1997). In addition, studies of social referencing indicate that children generally look to the adults in a room to help them understand what is expected of them (e.g., Boccia & Campos, 1989; Harari & McDavid, 1969).

Therefore, the DNE includes guidelines for coping with children's sensitivity to feedback and their potential need for a caregiver's or support person's presence in the room. For example, when separation anxiety is insurmountable, the interviewer instructs support persons to sit behind the child and to refrain from advising the child, instead redirecting the child back to the interviewer if the child is confused or has questions. Support persons might remain present during preliminaries and then try to leave before substantive questions begin. Given these findings and concerns about cross-contamination of witnesses and parental influence on children's reports, the DNE recommends interviewing children alone whenever possible.

In addition to social support, field studies are beginning to suggest that time spent developing rapport with children can improve their performance (Hershkowitz, 2009). Although more research is needed on the effectiveness of different rapport-building activities to accomplish greater trust, cooperation, honesty, or motivation, one field study did compare 50 children who failed to disclose validated instances of abuse with cooperative children who did disclose abuse (Hershkowitz,

Orbach, Lamb, Sternberg, & Horowitz, 2006). Children's responsiveness and engagement during rapport building were predictive of disclosure (Hershkowitz, 2011). There was some evidence that children who seemed reluctant and uncommunicative might be more willing to talk to the interviewer more freely when rapport building included support and open-ended prompts. In addition, there is some evidence to suggest that rapport development need not take long, probably under eight to ten minutes, and perhaps that lengthy rapport building might be counterproductive for some children, given young children's limited attention span overall (Davies, Westcott, & Horan, 2000).

Hence, in addition to recommendations for providing social support, the DNE

(a) includes time and activities for developing rapport prior to the core interview. Rapport-building time functions as an opportunity to

   (i)   break the ice and convey that the interviewer wants to get to know the child better and find out what people/activities are important to the child;

   (ii) use initial conversation to create a template for later questioning, demonstrating that interviewers are listeners, not interrogators, and that children are to provide as much accurate information as they can in their own words with minimal prompting; and

   (iii) listen to a child's grammar and vocabulary to be able to adjust your own language in later questioning to the child's developmental level.

(b) The DNE also provides suggestions and activities for overcoming children's anxiety and reluctance that are designed to be objective and convey understanding and respect for the child's thoughts and feelings without agreeing with the veracity of his or her account.

(c) Finally, the closure phase of the DNE includes suggestions for anticipating children's concerns about difficulties that could arise subsequent to the interview, and for planning positive coping strategies.

In closing our introduction to the DNE interview, we want to high-light five general principles for the reader's consideration that are woven throughout our approach:

1. Developmental Sensitivity

2. Forensic Justifiability

3. Objectivity

4. Flexibility

5. Empathy

Developmental Sensitivity

Beyond the use of the DNE procedure outlined in this guide, we encourage interviewers to adopt a developmental framework to their work overall; that is, to take a child's phase of development into account not only when phrasing questions, but when interpreting answers and using their discretion. A developmental framework can help determine how much weight to give an answer, or when to disregard the answer completely because the child does not possess the knowledge or skill to answer the question. It can provide a rationale for choosing one method over another and help the interviewer decide when to pursue, when to ease up, and when to terminate or reschedule. It also helps confirm or disconfirm one interpretation over another, untangling inconsistencies and alternative hypotheses. Such a framework can help predict what kind of witness a child will make and what accommodations might be necessary in court.

Forensic Justifiability

Forensic interviewers must expect their work to be scrutinized and even challenged in court, and they must be able to justify and defend their methods and choices. Court decisions can rest on the way the child was interviewed (e.g., U.S. Supreme Court decision in *Idaho v. Wright*,

1990). Remember that it will be a defense attorney's responsibility to raise doubts about children's credibility, and this is often accomplished by undermining the integrity of the interview and the impartiality of the interviewer. Cross-examination of interviewers can turn on an interviewer's failure to consider the pros and cons of various precautions and methods, even if the child's report was not actually contaminated. Substandard methods are legitimate targets for defense attorneys and defense experts.

Hence, we encourage interviewers to remember that, although only a small proportion of cases requires interviewers to testify, it is impossible to identify these cases in advance. So, it is incumbent upon the interviewer to stay current with the clinical and research literature and develop routine procedures that can be justified in court. When exceptions to routine procedures are necessary, and they often are, the interviewer must be able to articulate well-reasoned rationales on the stand. Routines should be based on familiarity with the literature, rules of evidence, and local standards of care and legal practices.

Objectivity

No witness is immune to the suggestions and biases of the interviewer, no matter what their age. Yet, young children, especially preschoolers, are a unique group. Their suggestibility and resistance to misleading information depends on children's current development in terms of their knowledge base, language comprehension, reasoning ability, social skills, emotional maturity, and memory ability (see Goodman & Melinder, 2007, for review). Hence, with all witnesses, but with younger children especially, the need for objectivity is clear. We urge interviewers to take on a role of ignorance and encourage children to take on the role of expert, emphasizing that the interviewer strives to understand the child's experience from his or her point of view, deliberately setting aside, as much as possible, preconceived hypotheses. Also, the interviewer is encouraged to be cognizant of the myriad ways in which his or her preconceptions, demeanor, behavior, and questions, as well as the circumstances of the interview, can inadvertently influence the child's statements. The child should feel that the interviewer is willing to accept as much or as little information as the child has to offer. Implementing the principle of objectivity means operating in a neutral fashion towards the veracity of the child's accounts, and conducting the interview in a nonjudgmental manner. Interviewers need to be aware of the insidious effects of bias and presumption, while considering multiple explanations and sides of an issue.

Flexibility

As with any evidence-based approach that is tested under highly controlled conditions, this guidebook outlines precise procedures. However, an underlying premise of our work is that interviewers need the flexibility to accommodate not only developmental differences among children, but also individual differences in children within the same age range. For example, a five-year-old boy who is depressed may appear to be withdrawn, indifferent, and slow to respond, if he responds at all; whereas a five-year-old boy with Attention Deficit Hyperactivity Disorder could be out of his seat more than in, off task more than on, distracted by every little noise in the hall or intriguing gadget on the desk, barely stopping to listen to a question. The interviewer needs the flexibility to apply different techniques to gain the cooperation and optimize the performance of these two very different children of the same age. Thus, the DNE is specifically designed to be used as a kind of "tool box" full of different techniques that the interviewer can use or not use, depending on individual characteristics or developmental limitations of the specific child being interviewed.

In addition, we understand that flexibility and discretion are necessary to accommodate to case-specific circumstances and varied agency goals and requirements. For example, some cases place heavy demands on children's memories, requiring recall of details that happened long ago. Other cases are more recent and include corroborating evidence. In the latter situations, a child need only provide the central events from a fresh memory, making for a less taxing interview and requiring fewer specific questions. Also, the purpose of an interview varies, demanding the flexibility to accommodate to various goals. Some questions are reasonable and necessary when the interview goal is to determine whether a child is in imminent danger and needs out-of-home placement that day.

But such questions may be controversial when time and physical danger are not of the essence.

Empathy

Finally, we encourage interviewers to make a conscious effort to maintain a child's dignity throughout. Just like adults, children respond to being treated with respect. The interviewer can show understanding for a child's situation without contaminating the child's testimony. Although the interviewer should not rely on assumptions or inferences, he or she can respond to a child's statement of how he or she feels or what is worrisome. If the interviewer acknowledges rather than minimizes or devalues a child's stated feelings, she can promote the communication process. Moreover, the interviewer can preserve or even enhance a child's motivation for cooperating with the next steps of the legal process.

The majority of recommendations in this guide are variations on these five principles as they are implemented in the DNE interview.

Alternative Approaches

A number of alternative approaches to forensic child-interviewing exist. Alternatives vary across nations and jurisdictions, from lists of best-practice guidelines promulgated by governmental agencies, to specific techniques tested in rigorous experiments with random assignment. Elsewhere we have described a list of research-derived principles and alternative protocols (Saywitz & Camparo, 2009). In the United States, for example, a number of well-known organizations (e.g., National Association of Child Advocacy Centers) and institutions (e.g., CornerHouse Interagency Child Abuse Evaluation and Training Center) have developed their own interview protocols for use in their own agencies. In contrast, New Zealand has passed legislation establishing a nationwide standard and infrastructure with a single training program and protocol for the entire nation (Wilson, 2007). One of the largest interview training programs in the United States, Finding Words, developed by the American Prosecutors Research Institute and the National Center for Prosecution of Child Abuse (in conjunction with CornerHouse) is a five-day course designed for multidisciplinary teams of front-line child abuse professionals.

Evidence-based alternatives to the DNE interview that have been subjected to rigorous testing with randomized trials are few. As reviewed in the following chapter, the components of the DNE have been tested with over 1000 children in experimental trials using random assignment. One other such evidence-based interview is the Cognitive Interview (CI). CI was first developed for use with adult witnesses by police officers, and it has shown beneficial results with adults in rigorous experimental studies in several countries. It is used widely in the field of law enforcement with adults. CI has since been tested with child witnesses in a number of randomized trials in the United States and United Kingdom (e.g., Saywitz, Geiselman, & Bornstein, 1992; McCauley & Fisher; 1995; Milne & Bull, 2003). CI uses four basic memory-jogging strategies derived from cognitive science to help witnesses recall details. Results with young children have been mixed, in that some of the components have been helpful to children (context reinstatement) and some problematic (change perspective task) (Brown & Pipe, 2003a; Memon, Wark, Bull, & Koehnken, 1997). We recommend that interested readers review the relevant literature to understand how to best implement CI with young children.

Additionally, the National Institute of Child Health and Human Development (NICHD) Investigative Interview Protocol, a set of structured guidelines for interviewing children in cases of suspected abuse, has been studied extensively in the field in the United States, United Kingdom, Canada, and Israel (Lamb et al., 2007). This protocol, like the DNE, is not a downward extension of an adult interview, but was specifically developed to be used with children. Its guidelines are generated from the experimental research on child eyewitness memory. As of this writing, we are not aware of any published studies with randomized trials; however, ample field-implementation studies suggest that when interviewers follow the NICHD protocol it helps them provide a more structured interview, for example, using three times more open-ended questions and half the number of suggestive questions than interviewers in the field without the protocol, improving the quality of children's reports. However, it is difficult for field researchers to evaluate effects of their protocol on accuracy or completeness of children's memory directly because they rarely know what actually occurred during alleged abuse crimes in the field. Hence, we recommend that readers follow the ongoing research to determine how best to apply the NICHD protocol to their work.

How to Use This Book

Our hope is that novice interviewers will learn the basics of evidence-based interviewing from this book, while more experienced interviewers will be able to add the Developmental Narrative Elaboration approach to their repertoire. In preparing this guide, we have done our best to present the techniques we have investigated in a usable form embedded in an interview template derived from our review of the available research with attention to the emerging consensus on best-practice recommendations among professional organizations. The suggestions in this guide are part of an ongoing conversation as data accumulate and the evidence base evolves. Readers will need to stay abreast of future research as they develop their own expertise on evidence-based child interviewing in the forensic context.

In Chapter 2, we provide readers with a detailed review of the experimental research that is the evidence base for the DNE interview. Chapter 3 begins our description of the step-by-step interview process with a discussion of how to set up the physical and psycho-social setting. Chapter 4 describes introductions; explanations of roles, purpose, and mechanics; developing rapport; coping with reluctance or anxiety; and using initial conversation to establish a template for later questioning. Chapter 5 discusses methods for demystifying the legal process when necessary and pointers that can raise children's awareness of the unique task demands of the interview. Chapters 6 and 7 describe optional techniques to promote children's performance that interviewers can choose to employ when they deem appropriate and time allows. When interviewers decide not to use the optional techniques in Chapters 6 and 7, they can proceed directly to the core interview as described in Chapter 8, which details the three steps for eliciting children's statements. Chapter 9 illustrates how to apply these three steps in cases of suspected child abuse and neglect. Finally, Chapter 10 discusses how to close the interview in a developmentally sensitive fashion.

Chapter 2   *Evidence Base for the Developmental Narrative Elaboration Interview*

What Is the Developmental Narrative Elaboration Interview Based On?

First and foremost, our goal has been to design and test an interview procedure that elicits reliable and complete information without tainting children's reports. To this end, the development of the DNE has relied heavily on an expansive and long-standing research base of normative trends in child development (e.g., Damon & Lerner, 2006). This literature comprises both cross-sectional studies that compare the development of an ability or skill across varied age groups (e.g., comparing memories of first, third, and fifth graders for the same event) and prospective longitudinal studies that follow the same group of children over time (e.g., testing the same group of children at three time points: for example, every year over a three-year period) to determine within which age range and under what conditions mastery emerges.

Second, we have relied heavily on the past 25 years of research on child forensic interviewing (e.g., Cronch, Viljoen, & Hansen, 2006; Goodman & Melinder, 2007; Perona, Bottoms, & Sorenson, 2006). This research base is composed of highly controlled laboratory-based analogue studies complemented by a rich body of field studies. The laboratory-based analogue studies typically involve staging an event or creating an activity that a community-based sample of children participate in, randomly assigning the children to different interview conditions, and then interviewing the children individually after a specific time delay. Researchers compare reports from children who have been interviewed with different question types, techniques, or protocols. Because the target event or activity has been staged and documented (e.g., videotaped), researchers are able to examine the accuracy (or inaccuracy) and completeness of the children's reports, comparing children's interview responses across the different interview formats to the documentation. Additionally, researchers have interviewed children about fictitious events using various interview techniques to compare the risk of false reports generated by each. Also, researchers have taken advantage of naturally occurring stressful events, such as an emergency room treatment for serious injury, by comparing children's recall to medical records and their parents' reports of the injury (e.g., Peterson & Bell, 1996; Peterson & Whalen, 2001).

This database is strengthened by the results of field studies that typically involve children who are alleged victims or witnesses of a crime (e.g., sexual abuse). Child forensic interviewers are trained to employ experimental techniques in the field, then researchers analyze transcripts by comparing the amounts of information the children provide and the types of questions the interviewers pose. Typically, field researchers cannot directly examine the completeness and accuracy of children's responses due to the fact that researchers may not know what actually occurred during alleged sexual-abuse crimes (however, see Bidrose & Goodman, 2000; and Leander, Christianson, & Granhag, 2007, for just two important exceptions to this limitation). Instead, they determine the efficacy of the interview protocol indirectly. They do so by examining the proportion of details elicited from children, as well as interviewers' use of techniques that have been found in laboratory research to elicit more complete and accurate responses from children (i.e., proportion of open-ended invitations vs. option-posing, directive, leading, and suggestive utterances). Taken together, results of laboratory-analogue studies and field research provide ample evidence for a wide array of research-based interview guidelines.

The final source of evidence on which we have relied is the results of our own studies and those of colleagues in other laboratories testing our techniques—for enhancing recall, communication, and resistance to suggestion—that make the DNE interview unique. In the sections that follow, we summarize the development and efficacy of the techniques employed in the DNE interview itself.

The Narrative Elaboration procedure is the heart of the DNE. This method has been studied with over 1,000 children ranging in age from three to 12. It has been tested with preschoolers (Bowen & Howie, 2002; Dorado & Saywitz, 2001) and children in elementary school (Brown & Pipe, 2003a; Brown & Pipe, 2003b; Camparo, Wagner, & Saywitz, 2001; Saywitz & Snyder, 1996; Saywitz, Snyder, & Lamphear, 1996) over retention intervals ranging from two weeks to nine months (Brown & Pipe, 2003a), regarding memory for staged classroom events (Bowen & Howie, 2002; Saywitz & Snyder, 1996), field trips, and highly stressful naturally occurring events like injuries requiring emergency room treatment (Peterson, Warren, & Hayes, 2013), as well as fictitious events to test suggestibility effects (Camparo et al., 2001). It has been studied in children with learning disabilities (Nathanson, Crank, Saywitz, & Ruegg, 2007) and children with varied levels of intelligence (Brown & Pipe, 2003b) and socio-economic status (Dorado & Saywitz, 2001). Studies have been conducted in our own laboratories in southern California and extended to other laboratories in the United States, Australia, New Zealand, and Canada.

In addition to the central Narrative Elaboration procedure, the DNE contains two optional elements. The first is an optional instruction and procedure to avoid miscommunications with young children by facilitating children's comprehension-monitoring and communication-response strategies (Saywitz, Snyder, & Nathanson, 1999; Peters & Nunez, 1999). The second is an optional instruction and procedure to increase children's resistance to misleading questions (Hershkowitz, 2011; Krakow & Lynn, 2009; Memon & Vartoukian, 1996; Saywitz & Moan-Hardie, 1994).

Also, the DNE includes a number of developmentally sensitive explanations of the forensic context, including the child's role, the interviewer's role, the information-gathering aspects of the investigative process, and relevant elements of adjudication that are derived from our studies of children's knowledge of the legal system and preparing them for court (e.g., Nathanson & Saywitz, 2003; Saywitz, 1989; Saywitz et al., 1990; Saywitz & Nathanson, 1993b; also see Quas & Sumaroka, 2011, for a recent review). In the sections that follow, we highlight the findings of these studies and the evolution of the DNE interview.

Evolution of the Narrative Elaboration Techniques

The Narrative Elaboration (NE) procedure was originally developed by Saywitz and Snyder (1996) for use with elementary school–age children. The procedure was revised in a follow-up replication study by Saywitz et al. (1996) designed to isolate some of the active ingredients responsible for the outcome. In both studies, children participated in a staged classroom event, and two weeks later, children were randomly assigned to participate in either NE or control activities prior to an interview that tested their recall for the classroom event. Control activities were carefully constructed to involve the same amount of time spent with the same interviewers engaging children in similar cognitive and memory tasks and stimuli. Analyses compared accuracy, completeness, and content of children's memories to the videotape of the event. The memories of children participating in the NE procedure were compared to the memories of children participating in various control groups in order to identify which component(s) of the NE interview made the greatest contribution to the outcome.

In the original study by Saywitz and Snyder (1996), 132 children from two age groups (seven- to eight-year-olds and 10- to 11-year-olds) were randomly assigned to one of three conditions: (a) NE intervention, (b) Instructions to be accurate and complete (I), or (c) a control group (see Saywitz & Snyder, 1996, for details). In the NE condition, children were given a *rationale* for using a new strategy to enhance performance and *instructions* to be complete and accurate. Then they were taught to use the *NE strategy:* Children were introduced to five visual cues, referred to as "reminder cards," to help them organize their narratives around five categories of forensically relevant information: Participants, Settings, Actions, Conversations/Affective States, and Consequences. Each card displayed a generic line drawing that represented the category (see "reminder cards" in Appendix A). While children *practiced* using the reminder cards on mock recall tasks,[1] the interviewer *modeled* how children could elaborate on their initial response by providing a few additional pieces of information from each category. This step conveys the kind of information and level of detail interviewers expect. Also, interviewers provided corrective *feedback* while cautioning children not to guess or push themselves to recall details about which they were unsure.

All the children were then interviewed about the classroom event individually and received the same instructions and interview questions. The interviewers followed a standardized protocol involving three recall tasks: (a) free recall; (b) cued-elaboration recall, in which children were shown each reminder card individually and asked if the card reminded them to tell anything more; and (c) probed recall, in which the children were asked the same set of prewritten short-answer questions about the staged event formulated according to DNE guidelines for developmental sensitivity. Children's reports were compared to a propositional analysis (Kintsch & Van Dijk, 1978) of the videotaped event that resulted in a checklist of 450 propositions of information (see Saywitz et al., 1996, for details).

Findings from Saywitz and Snyder's (1996) study indicated that the instructions to be complete and accurate were not effective when presented alone without the NE procedure; however, the children in the NE-intervention group demonstrated a significant increase in accurate information over the children in both control groups. In fact, in the Saywitz et al. (1996) study, 94% of the additional information obtained with the NE procedure was accurate. Analyses also indicated that the additional information reported as a result of the NE intervention was enhanced in both complexity (main ideas) and in richness (details). Also noteworthy, findings indicated that gains in the amount of accurate information in the NE condition were not offset by any increase in inaccurate information in the NE condition (Saywitz & Snyder, 1996; Saywitz et al., 1996). In both studies, results indicated there were no significant differences between the NE and control groups in inaccurate information during any of the three recall tasks.

Regarding analyses of how NE training might interact with age, Saywitz and Snyder (1996) found that, although the older children in their study generally recalled a significantly greater amount of accurate information and made significantly fewer errors than the younger children did, the effects of the NE intervention were beneficial for both the younger and older children. In fact, younger children using the NE procedure demonstrated recall comparable to that of the older children in the control group. This finding is particularly important because younger children are most likely to produce skeletal narratives requiring follow-up questions for clarification, and they are also least able to resist when follow-up questions are suggestive. Hence, they may benefit most from help in providing a larger store of reliable information in their own words on which to base follow-up questions.

Analyses of components of the NE by Saywitz and Snyder (1996) revealed that the consequences cue card was not effective. Since the consequences card had been the last card presented to the children, Saywitz et al. (1996) included a control group where category cues were presented in random order to examine whether the non-significant effect of the consequences card was due to fatigue. However, the consequences cue card was again ineffective, regardless of position. Moreover, although the absolute number of errors in both studies was small and the differences between the NE and the control groups were not significant, 75% of the errors made by the children in the NE group were in response to the consequences cue card. Hence, the consequences category cue card was eliminated in all further studies and the final version of the NE procedure.

Also noteworthy is the fact that in two subsequent studies, researchers tested the effects of the visual cards during the interview without giving children training and practice beforehand (Brown & Pipe, 2003b; Dorado & Saywitz, 2001). They found that the training and practice were necessary to obtain the full benefit of NE. The cards alone were insufficient. In fact, when children did not have the training and practice beforehand, some children occasionally made stimulus-bound errors in response to some of the cards, although these were easy for interviewers to identify and disregard. Hence, this guide cautions interviewers not to use the visual cue cards during the interview unless preceded by the training during the preliminary phase.

Adapting NE for Preschoolers

The NE procedure was adapted for preschoolers by a number of research teams. First, Dorado and Saywitz (2001) conducted a preliminary study of 40 four- to five-year-olds and then a more extensive study of an additional 99 four- to five-year-olds. Modifications involved simplifying the reminder card drawings to reduce stimulus-bound responses (see Appendix B), as well as modifying the rationale and the way the cards were introduced. Then Bowen and Howie (2002) tested a briefer NE procedure (see more detailed discussion in next section) with 72 four- to six-year-olds. Later, Peterson et al. (2013) included preschoolers as young as three years of age in their sample of 52 three-to-seven year olds, extending the age range further downward.

Consistent with the research on school-age children, results from these research teams indicated that preschoolers in the NE groups reported a significantly greater amount of accurate, but not inaccurate information, than children in the control groups. On average, preschoolers using the NE approach have produced more than twice as much accurate information overall (Bowen & Howie, 2002) and during cued-elaboration (Dorado & Saywitz, 2001) as did preschoolers in the control group. Remarkably, the preschoolers produced very little inaccurate information. Although preschoolers did make quite a few off-task (e.g., "I like your nail polish") and vague (e.g., "We played") remarks, children in the NE group did not produce significantly more irrelevant or vague remarks than the control group. When off-task, irrelevant comments were made, it was not difficult for interviewers to identify them and redirect preschoolers to the task at hand.

Thus, in the final version of the NE described in this guide, readers will find both a variation for preschoolers and a variation for elementary school–aged children, as well as tips for using the DNE with preschoolers derived from this research.

Streamlining the Narrative Elaboration

Although quite effective, the original NE procedure included several elements that made it difficult to use in the field. Hence, a number of research teams have tested streamlined versions of the procedure (Bowen & Howie, 2002; Brown & Pipe, 2003b; Camparo et al., 2001). The good news is that, despite variations in staged events, rationales, practice-recall tasks, length of delay between the event and recall interview, and amount of practice, the streamlined versions have all yielded results similar to those of the original studies—children provided increased accurate information without significant increases in errors when using the NE procedure—and this fact has remained true despite variations in the procedure across different studies by different research teams in different laboratories.

Camparo et al. (2001) developed a "streamlined" version that requires approximately 20 minutes to administer, combines the original teaching steps into one step with one practice task, and requires no additional materials or equipment. Practice focuses on retelling what the interviewer and child have done together thus far, while the interviewer demonstrates how the child can provide a few more pieces of information about each category and provides corrective feedback.

Bowen and Howie (2002) developed a "brief narrative elaboration" that is similar to the "streamlined" version developed by Camparo et al. (2001), except that they used a different practice task (recall of a picture-book story). Similar to all the previous studies, the information provided by the children during the practice was verifiable by the interviewer and thus open to interviewer elaboration and corrective feedback.

Finally, Brown and Pipe (2003b) also tested a modification with seven- to eight-year-olds that eliminates the visual cue cards (i.e., reminder cards) and the training and practice altogether. This version, referred to as Verbal Labels (VL), replaces visual cues during the cued-recall task with four open-ended verbal prompts about the same four categories of information (e.g., "Tell me more about the people who were there and how they looked"). Brown and Pipe (2003b) compared the VL group's performance on the memory interview to the original NE protocol using visual cues (Saywitz & Snyder, 1996) and to a control group (who received no training and no verbal category prompts, but were shown the NE visual cue cards after the free-recall task and asked, "Does this card help you to tell something else about [the target event]?").

Consistent with the results of the original studies, all three studies of a shortened version found significant increases in the amount of accurate information—but not the amount of inaccurate information—over standard protocols or control conditions and the effects were quite robust despite considerable variation in the procedure across studies. In particular, in the Brown and Pipe (2003b) study, children responding to the verbal cues performed comparably to children who had received the original NE training with visual cues. These findings suggest that perhaps the most important component of the NE procedure is the extra opportunity for category-cued elaboration (whether visual or verbal) inserted after free recall and prior to follow-up questioning during the interview. In all of the studies reviewed thus far, the information that children provided in response to open-ended unbiased prompts prior to specific follow-up questions (free recall plus cued recall),[2] was expanded significantly, creating a larger base of reliable information from which interviewers could construct follow-up questions, thereby reducing the potential for leading questions and contamination.

Hence, the final version of the NE procedure detailed in this guide is a brief, streamlined version with two variations: (a) the NE procedure with streamlined training, practice, and visual cue cards for children of all ages between three and 12; and (b) the NE procedure with verbal cues that forgoes the practice in the preliminary phase and substitutes the verbal cues tested by Brown and Pipe (2003b) for the visual cue cards during the interview. Although the verbal-cue variation is based heavily, but not solely, on the results of this one study of typically developing seven- to eight-year-olds' recall of a single staged event, several other researchers have found increased information without increased errors in response to similar verbal category cues with children three to eight years of age (Elischberger & Roebers, 2001; Kulkofsky, 2010; Poole & Lindsay, 1995).[3] Hence, it is reasonable to infer that even young children will benefit from the verbal cue option. Therefore, when time is of the essence or children lack the attentional resources, the verbal-cue option is available. However, further research is needed to test the verbal-cue option with younger children and with fictitious and "real-life" events. In Chapter 6 we discuss when it might be best to use the visual cue-card option and when to use the verbal-cue option. In Chapter 8, describing the core interview, we present both options.

Does the Narrative Elaboration Lead Children to Report More Erroneous Information When Interviewed About a Fictitious Event?

Ironically, the consistent finding that the NE significantly enhances the amount of information children report raised a very serious concern: Does the NE also lead children to report more information about an event that we know did *not* happen? To address this concern, Camparo et al. (2001) asked children to report about both a staged field-trip event and a fictitious field trip to the desert. Ninety-two first- to sixth-grade children were interviewed about both events in counterbalanced order, using either the streamlined NE, a control condition that provided the children with the cards during the interview but not advance training in the use of the cue cards (NE cards–no training group), or a standard protocol (SP) of free recall followed by a series of follow-up questions (SP group).

Results indicated there were no group differences in the amount of false information reported about the fictitious event. Surprisingly, 98% of all the children denied experiencing the fictitious event when asked the first of three free-recall prompts about the field trip. Only five children provided some false information at any point in the interview: two were from the NE group and three were from the control groups.[4] Two of these children's reports were telling: One child provided no information in response to either the free recall or cue-card prompts, but when the interviewer continued to ask a series of follow-up questions about the fictitious event anyway, he provided 906 pieces of (inaccurate) information in response to the probed questions about the fictitious event. The second child repeatedly denied experiencing the fictitious event during all three free-recall prompts; however, when the interviewer proceeded to question the child about the field trip anyway, she responded to the category cue card with, "You mean, even if I didn't go?" When the interviewer did not answer, the child proceeded to provide 520 pieces of (inaccurate) information about the fictitious event over the remainder of the interview. These two children highlight the rare but serious danger of ignoring children's denials or implying, through repeated prompting or silence, that they should answer questions about events they deny occurred.

Does the Narrative Elaboration Enhance Children's Narratives of Emotionally Charged Real-Life Events?

Another concern raised by methodological limitations of the research testing the efficacy of the NE was that the NE may only be useful for enhancing children's recall of "child-friendly" staged events. To address this limitation, a Canadian study examined the efficacy of the NE protocol for eliciting three- to seven-year-old children's autobiographical reports of a highly stressful and personally salient real-life event (Peterson et al., 2013). In this study, the event was a recent injury sustained by the child that was serious enough to require emergency room medical treatment (e.g., broken bone, laceration requiring sutures). Because previous findings have indicated that children's recall for highly salient, emotionally charged, and unique events—properties that characterize many forensic events—is already quite accurate and fairly complete (e.g., Peterson & Warren, 2009), use of such a target event provides invaluable information regarding the efficacy of the NE protocol under such real-world circumstances. Moreover, unlike most real-world cases of sexual or physical abuse, facts surrounding an injury that requires medical treatment can be verified. Thus, both the accuracy and the completeness of the children's reports may be determined.

Peterson et al. (2013) used a version of the NE protocol most similar to Bowen and Howie's (2002), including four reminder cards and one practice task with a children's book. Children in the NE condition were compared to children in a "standardized interview" that was composed of a free-recall prompt followed by a list of prewritten general questions about their injury following the guidelines from the NICHD Investigative Interviewing Protocol described by Sternberg et al. (1996) to avoid leading or suggestive questions. (e.g., "How did it happen?" "Who was the first person who came and got you?" "Where were you when it happened?").

Consistent with previous research, results indicated that children in the NE group provided a significantly greater amount of correct information in response to open-ended recall (free recall plus cued recall) than did the children in the control group (free recall only), with no significant difference in the amount of incorrect information provided by each group. Specifically, this difference translated to a 59% improvement over the control group in recall for a highly stressful personal event where a child was injured, without the use of potentially leading questions, meaning that if the probed questions used in the study had not been prewritten and standardized for the two groups, the interviewers in the NE condition would have had a significantly greater amount of accurate information on which to base their follow-up questions than the interviewers in the control condition would have had.

Narrative Elaboration Enhances Narratives of Children from Middle and Low Socio-Economic Status Levels

Dorado and Saywitz (2001) compared reports from children recruited from federal- and state-subsidized preschools that required participating families to have incomes near or below the poverty level to the reports of children recruited from private preschools in adjacent communities that required tuition payments of $100 per week or more. Analyses demonstrated that the benefits of NE training were significant for both middle- and low-SES children. In this study, 76% of children from the low SES communities were ethnic minorities. This is important because, although child abuse occurs at all socioeconomic levels, low-SES families are over-represented in reported cases of abuse (Steinmetz, 1971; Straus, Gelles, & Steinmetz, 1980). Therefore, any technique used with children in suspected child-abuse cases must be demonstrated to be useful and culturally appropriate for children from low-SES and ethnic minority communities. Low-SES preschoolers in the NE group produced nearly 2½ times more accurate information during cued elaboration than did low-SES children in the control group. Dorado and Saywitz's (2001) findings are particularly noteworthy because they allow us to extend the benefits of NE to children from low-SES communities who were predominately from ethnic minority backgrounds.

Narrative Elaboration Is Effective over Long Delays

Although most of the studies of NE have tested its efficacy for events recalled for a matter of weeks, Brown and Pipe (2003a) examined the efficacy of NE over a nine-month delay. They compared memories of children interviewed with NE to those of a control group, both two weeks after a staged event (47 six- to eight-year-olds) and nine months after the same event (22 six- to eight-year-olds). After the two-week delay, children in the NE condition reported more correct information and were more accurate in their reports than children in the control condition. Even after the nine-month delay, children in the NE condition reported significantly more correct information than did children in the control group during cued-elaboration (primarily information about participants and setting), and it was not at the expense of overall accuracy. In fact, children in the NE condition reported 55% more information overall than did controls nine months after the event, and again, the additional details were reported during the cued-recall phase of the interview.

Consistent with previous research, there were no group differences in overall amount of erroneous information or answers to specific follow-up questions (Brown & Pipe, 2003a). However, children in the NE condition did make more errors in describing participants' clothing (though not their identities) after a nine-month delay, and interviewers should exercise caution when determining the significance of children's descriptions of attire over long delays.

Narrative Elaboration Improves the Quality of Information from Children

Although the amount and accuracy of information has obvious benefits for the investigative phase of any criminal case, the descriptive detail, coherence (i.e., use of appropriate conjunctions, disjunctions, and other connectors within sentences), and references to locations in the child's report have a profound impact on perceptions of the child's credibility. Researchers find that more fully elaborated witness reports are rated as more credible by mock jurors (Bell & Loftus, 2006), and it is thought that children who provide such accounts are more likely to be believed as witnesses (Bala, Lee, & McNamara, 2001; Peterson et al., 2013). Findings from one recent study suggest that childhood memories of real events are more fully elaborated than reports of imagined events (Krackow, 2010). Moreover, researchers have found that children who provided more descriptive reports about a staged event were also more resistant to suggestive questioning about that same staged event, and that narrative quality superseded age as a predictor of such resistance (Kulkofsky & Klemfuss, 2008).

Consequently, to explore differences in the quality of children's narratives when using the NE versus a standard interview protocol, Camparo and Camparo (2011) and Peterson et al. (2013) examined several qualities of children's narrative reports about a staged event (Camparo & Camparo,

2011) and a serious injury (Peterson et al., 2013) when interviewed with either the NE or a standard protocol. Camparo and Camparo (2011) focused on the descriptive quality of the narratives of 4–6, 7–9, and 10–12-year-olds, and Peterson et al. (2013) focused on causal connectives (e.g., "because," "if," "so"); temporal connectives ("first," "next," "later," "before," "after"); and contextual embedding (specification of location) of three- to seven-year-olds' narratives.

As predicted, results from both studies indicated that the quality of children's narrative reports was higher when using the NE interview than when using the standard interview. Camparo and Camparo (2011) found that, in response to open-ended questioning,[5] children interviewed with the NE provided seven times more accurate descriptors than did children interviewed with the standard protocol. Additionally, across the entire interview,[6] including specific follow-up questions, children interviewed with the NE provided nearly twice as many accurate descriptors as did children in the standard-interview group, with no significant differences in the number of inaccurate descriptors.[7]

As noted above, Peterson et al. (2013) examined the children's coherence and references to locations in their study and found that the NE elicited significantly more coherent sentences (use of conjunctions, disjunctions, and other connectors) and more references to locations in response to open-ended questions than did the standard protocol; however, there were no significant differences for causal (e.g., "because") or temporal (e.g., "then") connectives. Taken together, findings from these two studies suggest that the NE may serve to not only enhance the amount and accuracy of children's reports, but the *quality* of their narrative reports as well. Given that narrative quality may be more strongly associated than age with resistance to suggestive questioning about the same event and is associated with perceptions of greater credibility, these findings are particularly compelling.

Nevertheless, just as earlier research examining the volume of information elicited by the NE raised the question of whether or not the NE would be more likely to elicit false reports about a fictitious event, an important question to consider is whether the NE is more likely than a standard protocol to elicit higher quality narratives about a fictitious event. Again, given that more elaborately detailed narratives are perceived as being more credible, such an effect could be particularly damaging.

To explore this question, Normand, Camparo, and Almeria (2012) examined differences in the number of unique descriptors about a fictitious event provided by children interviewed using the NE versus a standard protocol. Using the same data as those used by Camparo and Camparo (2011), Normand et al. found that children interviewed with the NE did not provide significantly more unique descriptors about the fictitious event across the entire interview than did children interviewed with the standard interview.[8] Additionally, across the entire interview, an age by interview-condition interaction suggested that NE may actually serve a protective function for the older children. Older children interviewed with the NE provided significantly fewer descriptors about a fictitious event than did the younger children interviewed with the NE, whereas the older children interviewed with the standard interview provided more descriptors about the fictitious event than the younger children interviewed with the standard interview.

In sum, research indicates that NE helps children of all ages provide more accurate descriptors about a known event, and may serve a protective function for older children with regard to providing descriptors about a fictitious event without causing younger children to provide false descriptors about a fictitious event.

Narrative Elaboration Enhances the Narratives of Children with Learning Disabilities and Lower IQ Scores

Numerous studies have indicated that oral narration is more difficult for children with learning disabilities when compared to their non-disabled peers (e.g., Scott & Windsor, 2000). According to one theory, these children do not lack the abilities to give full narrative accounts; rather, they lack the strategies for organizing and delivering narratives (Deshler & Schumaker, 1993). Yet children with disabilities are at higher risk of victimization than are non-disabled children. Nathanson et al. (2007) hypothesized that children with learning disabilities[9] may be at a disadvantage in the forensic context and could benefit from the training and strategies employed in narrative elaboration. They tested the efficacy of NE with seven- to twelve-year-olds identified as learning-disabled by their school districts. The interview consisted of only open-ended questions—a free-recall task followed by the cued-elaboration task. As in other studies of NE, children with learning disabilities in the NE condition reported a significantly greater amount of accurate information overall than did children with learning disabilities in the control group. While the free recall of the two groups did not differ significantly, the results of the cued-recall task were remarkable. Children with learning disabilities in the NE condition reported almost eight times more additional, non-redundant, accurate information in cued recall than did children in the control group, without a significant difference in the amount of inaccurate information reported.

In addition, studies have found that the NE procedure is especially helpful to children who score lower on standard tests of intelligence. Brown and Pipe (2003b) found that performance on a standard interview protocol was predicted by children's IQ score—children with higher IQ scores (over the mean of 100 on the Wechsler Intelligence Test of Children) reported more correct information than did children with lower IQ scores (less than 100). However, there were no such differences when the NE procedure was employed. Both the NE visual-cue option and the NE verbal-cue option were especially effective for children of lower IQ scores. Moreover, the IQ differences seemed to be driven by the children's scores on the vocabulary subtest. We note this finding because it may suggest that the NE could be especially useful with children who have less facility with the language in which they are being interviewed. Hence, the NE procedure may be particularly useful, not only for children with learning disabilities and lower IQ scores, but also immigrants and bilingual children for whom the language of the interview is not their first or primary language. However, further research would be needed to confirm this inference.

Summary of Narrative Elaboration Research

Over the last 16 years of research, positive effects of NE have been demonstrated by different research teams in different countries testing over 1,000 children in randomized trials across short and long delays of up to nine months (Brown & Pipe, 2003a, 2003b; Camparo et al., 2001; Dorado & Saywitz, 2001; Saywitz & Snyder, 1996; Saywitz et al., 1996). NE has been found to be ecologically valid in studies of stressful life events, such as injuries requiring emergency room treatment (Peterson et al., 2012). The NE has been found to elicit more correct information without jeopardizing accuracy in every study in which it has been used. Accuracy rates for additional information gained in open-ended recall with NE are extremely high, typically in the 94% to 97% range (Peterson et al., 2013; Saywitz et al., 1996). In each study, NE provided the interviewer with a larger base of accurate information during the initial part of the interview in response to open-ended prompts on which to base follow-up questions. Since children produce a larger data source with NE from which to derive follow-up questions, the potential for increased error that accompanies more specific and potentially leading follow-up questions is reduced.

Consistently, researchers find NE works well for children traditionally considered difficult to interview. Although originally designed for school-age children, NE has also been adapted for preschoolers with positive effects seen in those as young as three years of age (Bowen & Howie, 2002; Dorado & Saywitz, 2001; Peterson et al., 2013) and children with learning disabilities (Nathanson et al., 2007). Additionally, it has been found to reduce the effect of lower IQ scores on children's ability to report details (Brown & Pipe, 2003b) and to benefit children from low-SES, predominately ethnic minority communities, and children with low vocabulary test scores, which might indicate less facility with the language in which they are being interviewed (Brown & Pipe, 2003b; Dorado & Saywitz, 2001). Moreover, it has been compared favorably to a cadre of control groups, including studies following the NICHD Investigative Interviewing Protocol guidelines (Peterson et al., 2012), and comparably to elements of the Cognitive Interview (CI) (e.g., context reinstatement) in terms of increased productivity (Bowen & Howie, 2002; Brown & Pipe, 2003a), although CI has shown mixed results across studies, with some researchers finding increased commission errors and confabulations (e.g., Memon et al., 1997).

In addition to enhancing the amount of accurate information in children's reports, NE also enhances the quality of children's narratives about both staged and emotionally charged real-life events (Camparo &

Camparo, 2011; Peterson et al., 2013). With NE, reports are enriched in main ideas and details. While children's free-recall narratives in response to standard protocols are primarily descriptions of central actions, the extra information children provide with NE adds details about the participants' identities, appearance, thoughts, utterances, emotions, behaviors, conversations, affective states, as well as details about the context, including location, setting descriptions, and objects present. Across the event categories, accuracy rates typically range from 100% to 87% (e.g., Brown & Pipe, 2003b). In addition, information elicited with NE has been classified as more coherent and credible than information elicited from control groups. Often, younger children using the NE procedure performed at the level of older children in the control groups.

Studies suggest a number of cautions as well, however. Children should not be asked to use the visual cue cards during an interview without first participating in the training during the preparatory phase (Brown & Pipe, 2003b; Dorado & Saywitz, 2001). In addition, if children deny they have experienced the relevant events, they should not be pushed with the NE cued-recall task to provide details. Interviewers should exercise caution in interpreting children's recall of people's attire using the visual reminder cards after long delays. And finally, interviewers should bear in mind that the visual reminder cards are more helpful for some children than others. There may be some children who do not report additional information in response to the visual reminder cards during the core interview.

Improving Communication Between Children and Interviewers

In addition to the overall template and the NE procedure, we tested an intervention designed to reduce miscommunication and improve the accuracy of children's interview performance. It is an optional component of the DNE detailed in Chapter 7. Although developmentally sensitive interviewers do their best to ask questions in a language children can understand, it is inevitable that children will be confronted by some adult questions containing vocabulary or grammar that are difficult for them to comprehend. Studies have shown that child witnesses are confronted frequently with developmentally inappropriate questions (e.g., Brennan and Brennan, 1988; Davies & Seymore, 1998; Evans et al., 2009).

Saywitz et al. (1999) developed and tested the efficacy of instructions and a brief pre-interview activity designed to increase children's awareness of instances of non-comprehension and to teach them strategies for eliciting a simpler rephrase from the interviewer when non-comprehension is detected. Saywitz, et al. (1999) randomly assigned 180 six- and eight-year-olds to three conditions: (a) Rephrase Instructions (RI): instructing children that some of the questions might be easy to understand, but some might be hard to understand, and instructing them to ask the interviewer to rephrase the question in simpler terms when they do not understand a question fully; (b) Comprehension Monitoring (CM): similar instructions as in RI, plus a pre-interview activity in which children practice detecting incomprehensible questions and practice asking for rephrasing with modeling and feedback; or (c) a control group given Motivating Instructions (MI) such as "Try your hardest. Do your best." The memory interview consisted of questions that varied from easy to difficult-to-comprehend.

Results indicated that both older and younger children in both the RI and the CM conditions provided a significantly greater number of correct answers and a significantly lower number of incorrect answers during the memory interview, compared with the children in the control group. The RI group made 20% fewer errors than the control group; however, the group who received CM practice made 56% fewer errors than the control group.

To evaluate the children's use of the strategies, Saywitz et al. (1999) examined specific responses to difficult-to-comprehend questions. When confronted with difficult-to-comprehend questions, children in the control group tried to answer anyway a majority of the time (71%), but were as likely to respond incorrectly as correctly. They rarely asked for clarification. In contrast, children who received the CM practice verbalized their lack of comprehension a majority of the time (73%) and provided correct answers to 81% of the questions across the entire interview. Children in the RI condition performed significantly better than the control group but significantly less well than the CM group. In summary, the CM training effectively cut the children's error rate on follow-up questions in half compared with the control group, providing strong support for continued use of the CM training in forensic contexts.

In addition, Peters and Nunez (1999) replicated these findings in a study of 99 preschoolers, kindergarteners, and second-graders, extending the age range downward to preschoolers. Their results showed significant benefits from CM training at each age group. Children in the CM condition were more likely to ask adults to rephrase complex questions and to answer rephrased questions correctly, whereas children in the control condition tended to try to answer the complex questions without asking for a rephrase. Hence, the DNE includes the Rephrase Instruction in our toolkit of instructions, since it is effective even without the training (Chapter 5), and the Comprehension Monitoring pre-interview practice activity, since it reduces error so dramatically and is more effective than instructions alone (Chapter 7). Both are viewed as optional components of the DNE.

Increasing Children's Resistance to Suggestion

In addition to the overall template and the NE and CM procedures, in two other studies we tested an intervention designed to increase children's resistance to misleading questions. Elements of this intervention are included as *optional* instructions (described in Chapter 5) and an optional pre-interview activity (described in Chapter 7). Elements of this intervention are also found in other contemporary interview protocols, such as the NICHD Investigative Interview protocol (Lamb, LaRooy, Malloy, & Katz, 2011) and Event Report Training (Krackow & Lynn, 2009). Also, some of these elements have been studied by other researchers in the laboratory (Cordón et al., 2005; Endres, Poggenpohl, & Erben, 1999; Geddie, Fradin, & Beer, 2000; Gee et al., 1999; Memon & Vartoukian, 1996; Moston, 1987; Walker, Lunning, & Eilts, 1996; Warren, Hulse-Trotter, & Tubbs, 1991).

In our own lab, we (Saywitz and Moan-Hardie, 1994) tested the efficacy of an intervention designed to (a) increase children's awareness of the task demands in forensic interviews, (b) make response options explicit, and (c) highlight the potential for negative consequences from acquiescence to suggestions or guessing. Across the two studies, a total of 102 second-grade children participated in a staged event and were interviewed later with misleading, correctly leading, and non-leading questions about specific information. Children in the intervention group were warned that they might not know all the answers, that some questions might be easy and others difficult, and that they should be on guard against adults' putting guesses into their questions inadvertently. They were reminded that the interviewer was not present at the event and therefore could not have firsthand knowledge about the event. Children were told to stop and think before answering (e.g., "Don't hurry into a wrong answer"); to replay the event internally and compare their memory to the adult's question; and to answer the question if they knew the answer, responding "I don't know" or "I don't remember" if they did not, or "That's wrong" if the interviewer made a mistake. Additionally, children were taught to use self-statements to promote confidence (e.g., "I knew there would be questions like this. I can do it"; "I won't go along. I'll tell her she's wrong"), and inhibit guessing (e.g., "I won't hurry into a wrong answer").

Results of Study 1 indicated that the intervention was successful in reducing false responses to misleading questions without increasing error on other types of questions (Saywitz & Moan-Hardie, 1994). However, the intervention also had the unintended effect of producing an overly cautious response set, so that the children over-generalized the "I don't know/remember" strategies to the correctly leading questions, resulting in fewer correct responses to these questions. Consequently, we (Saywitz and Moan-Hardie, 1994) conducted Study 2 on a new sample, this time placing greater emphasis on the children's providing substantive responses whenever they knew the answer to a question and less emphasis on admitting lack of knowledge. This solved the problem. The modified version did not have the adverse effect found in Study 1, and the children in the intervention group achieved a significantly greater reduction in errors on specific questions as well as on misleading questions. Hence, in the present guide, we include the instructions and key components from this study in our toolkit of optional techniques.

As further support, Krackow and Lynn (2009) included a number of these components in their experimental study of 58 children's recall of a staged event and found reduced suggestibility to abuse-related questions in preschoolers. Moreover, the NICHD Investigative Interview protocol, studied with thousands of children in the field, recommends giving children permission to say "I don't know/remember" and to correct the interviewer if necessary (Hershkowitz, 2011, p. 115). Thus, we include them as optional components of the DNE to be used at the interviewer's discretion.

Increasing Children's Awareness of the Forensic Context

Throughout the DNE procedure, you will see developmentally sensitive instructions and explanations that serve to demystify the legal system and address gaps in children's knowledge of the forensic context. These elements are derived from our studies of children's conceptions of the legal system (Saywitz, 1989), children's understanding of legal terminology (Saywitz et al., 1990), and preparing children for court (Nathanson & Saywitz, 2003; Saywitz & Nathanson, 1993b). Additionally, other researchers have found that lack of legal knowledge was related to distress when providing testimony (Goodman et al., 1998; Quas, Wallin, Horowitz, Davis, & Lyon, 2009; Sas et al., 1991) and when providing memory reports about staged events in mock-trial settings (Nathanson & Saywitz, 2003). Hence, the DNE includes these explanations in an effort to improve children's knowledge of the forensic context in the service of improving their performance and reducing the distress associated with the unknown or misunderstood.

We examined (Saywitz, 1989) 48 children's conceptions of the legal system: half the children were actively involved in legal cases as witnesses for at least three months and half were not involved in a legal case. We investigated children's understanding of the roles of the various legal professionals; witness credibility; awareness of the fact-finding, truth-telling, and decision-making processes; and children's abilities to distinguish between the investigative, penal, and judicial systems. Results demonstrated age-related trends. For example, we found that most four- to seven-year-olds demonstrated no awareness that the goal is to gather evidence and determine if it is the truth; they did not understand that evidence must be collected, presented to others, and evaluated (Saywitz, 1989). In contrast, older children, eight to 14 years of age, did have some understanding of the fact-finding and truth-finding aspects of the process; however, they still did not understand that the judge and jury are impartial and independent (e.g., many older children believed the judge and jury go into a room together and discuss the case).

We investigated 60 kindergarteners', third, and sixth graders' knowledge of legal terms gleaned from transcripts of child witness testimony in legal proceedings (Saywitz et al., 1990). Some terms showed significant age-related trends, including *fact, witness, case, truth, date, lawyer, hearing, parties, evidence, oath, identify,* and *testify*. Still, some of the legal terms were understood by virtually none of the children, including *allegations, petition, minor, motion, competent, hearsay, charges,* and *defendant*. Results of these two studies were similar to those of researchers in other laboratories (Perry et al., 1995; Warren-Leubecker et al., 1989) and in the field (Plotnikoff & Woolfson, 2009; Quas et al., 2009; Sas, Hurley, Hatch, Malla, & Dick, 1993). Moreover, limited understanding was often true even of older children and children with more extensive experience in the legal system (Quas et al., 2009; Saywitz, 1989).

In summary, all of these studies show age-related trends such that younger children are often unaware of the precise roles and responsibilities of legal professionals and the purpose of various legal procedures, including investigative interviews. While there is still a need for more research on children's understanding of the legal system, a number of court-education programs now exist in English-speaking countries, including the United States, England, Canada, and Australia. Studies have shown children can learn about the legal system when information is presented at their level of understanding. The developmentally sensitive explanations given to children in the DNE are based on the available research literature as well as the court-education and stress-reduction curriculum currently in use in Las Vegas, Nevada, that was developed by Saywitz and Nathanson (1993b).

Conclusions

The central goal of the DNE interview is to close the gap between the requirements of the forensic interview and the limitations of children's capabilities. This is accomplished by reducing the difficulty of the interview task downward towards the child's developmental level and providing children with memory and communication strategies to improve their performance. It is both a top-down and bottom-up approach.

Over the past 16 years of research, a solid base of evidence on the elements of the DNE has accumulated. The resulting DNE Interview described in this guide is an overall template for three phases of interviewing, with variations for children of different age groups and optional components to be deployed at the interviewer's discretion on a case-by-case basis. It is not a rigid script to be followed to the letter. Given the similar results across studies despite considerable variations in procedure by different research teams, this guide offers sample language, optional procedures, and alternative activities. Interviewers can use a streamlined, purely verbal version of the interview that requires no extra materials and no pre-interview training or practice activities. Or they can embed in the template a number of optional techniques that have been shown to improve children's completeness and accuracy, including the visual cues with practice. These techniques have been found to benefit children who are traditionally more difficult to interview, including younger children; children with learning disabilities, low IQ and vocabulary scores; and children from low-SES, ethnic minority communities. Readers are advised to keep abreast of ongoing and future research to guide application.

Over the course of the three phases of the DNE, interviewers make the task demands, interviewer expectations, and the forensic context explicit through developmentally sensitive explanations, instructions, modeling, and feedback. Interviewers provide the scaffolding necessary to guide the memory search toward forensically relevant categories of information and to address developmental limitations in the generation and deployment of retrieval strategies. The outcome is a more reliable and complete report, increased in both quantity and quality of information, without increased error. Children's initial narratives are more fully elaborated with relevant detail (in response to simple open-ended, unbiased prompts), providing interviewers with a larger data set of reliable information from which to craft better-informed, and potentially less biased, follow-up questions. In addition, the DNE includes the evidence-based guidelines utilized in our studies to formulate developmentally sensitive follow-up questions that avoid suggestive techniques and are phrased in language and concepts children can understand. In the ensuing chapters, we will detail the procedures and options of the three phases.

Phase I Preliminary Phase

Chapter 3

Before the Interview: Setting Up the Interview Context

Materials Needed

- Appropriate physical setting
- Video/audio equipment (optional)
- Note-taking materials

Outline

- Schedule the interview
- Set up the physical setting
- Create a supportive psycho-social setting
- Document the content and process of the interview

Introduction

One of the goals of Phase I of the Developmental Narrative Elaboration (DNE) interview is to create a context that facilitates, rather than undermines, the child's cooperation, motivation, and optimal performance. This chapter gives pointers on creating a physical, psychological, and social atmosphere that is developmentally sensitive to a child's needs. It also addresses how to establish rapport and set the ground rules while maintaining the objectivity so important for forensic justifiability.

Scheduling and Length of Interview

The length of the interview, including time devoted to introductions, developing rapport, going over explanations, and completing practice tasks, must be compatible with the individual child's developmental level, temperament, and coping skills. An interview places a number of cognitive, social, and emotional demands on children that can be difficult for them to meet for long periods of time, such as:

- sitting still

- paying close attention

- listening

- following instructions

- drawing meaning from the interviewer's questions

- recalling potentially confusing and emotionally upsetting details

- coping with emotions that arise

- verbally recounting events

Over the course of our studies, the DNE has been streamlined to accommodate children's developing abilities and skills. On average, interviews ranged from 20 to 30 minutes, excluding time for closure, which varies from child to child in the forensic context. In our experience, interviews in the field with older children who have a lot to say may take significantly longer.

The Setting

The Physical Setting

The DNE provides children with a safe, private, child-friendly setting, free of distraction. The following checklist can be used for creating an appropriate environment.

Physical Setting Checklist

✓ *Private:* Interview the child alone unless there is a good reason for allowing a support person to be present. To eliminate the potential for or appearance of cross-contamination, other witnesses (e.g., siblings) should not be present. Also ensure that the child's statements will not be heard by other witnesses/victims or persons with a stake in the case outcome (e.g., if they are waiting outside the room).

If a support person is necessary, strive to limit her presence to only the preliminary phase (Phase I) of the interview. Ask the support person to leave before the substantive questioning (Phase II) begins. Ask the support person to sit behind the child during Phase I and give the following instructions:

If [name of child] looks to you to help her answer a question, I want you to direct her back to me. You can tell her we are here to understand what she remembers (thinks, feels).

- *Tell her you cannot help her answer the questions.*
- *Tell her to try her best to answer the questions honestly and completely.*
- *Tell her that if she is confused or afraid she can ask me any questions she wants, and I will do my best to answer her honestly and completely, too.*

✓ *Safe*: Anticipate and address the child's safety concerns in advance of the interview (e.g., showing the child where caretakers will be waiting; telling adults in front of the child not to disturb the interview).

- When children express fears or have been threatened with punishment if they talk, avoid devaluing their feelings with statements like "Don't be worried." or "There's nothing to be afraid of." Instead, consider whether extra measures may be necessary, such as stationing a "guard" outside the door to reassure a child who has witnessed a sudden violent act that there will be no interruptions.

✓ *Minimal distractions*: Eliminate intriguing toys and other objects that will "pull" a child's attention away from the verbal exchange.

✓ *No interruptions*: Avoid answering phones or pagers so as not to derail a child's attention, and place a "Do Not Disturb" sign on the door.

✓ *Quiet*: Avoid noisy locations that will distract the child or make it difficult for you and the child to hear each other. Victims of abuse and trauma are often hypervigilant and easily startled by sudden, unexpected noises.

✓ *Age-appropriate and somewhat familiar*: Use a setting that is similar to settings a child would be familiar with (e.g., a playroom, small classroom, study room). Be aware, however, that interviewing the child in her home or at the scene of a crime can have serious drawbacks.

✓ *Child-sized furniture with non-thematic decorations*: Use appropriately sized, comfortable furniture; however, minimize elaborate decorations and technical equipment that may draw and hold the child's attention and interest.

✓ *Toys/interview aids*: Simplify materials used as aids during the interview—typically markers or crayons and paper are sufficient for breaking the ice and helping the child remain seated and relaxed during the interview.

✓ *Adequate time to acclimate*: Allow the child time to explore and ask questions about items in the room (e.g., one-way mirror, video equipment, pictures, etc.) before continuing with Phase I.

✓ *Interview schedule*: Schedule the interview during a time when the child is not tired or hungry (i.e., avoid nap and mealtimes) and will not miss cherished activities (e.g., soccer game).

The Psycho-social Setting

In addition to the physical setting, the interviewer must consider the psychosocial setting of the interview. Social support can help children be more resistant to misleading questions and improve their performance

INTERVIEW SETTING CHECKLIST

This checklist may be used to ensure that an appropriate environment is created for the interview. Refer to the preceding text for detailed instructions.

Physical Setting

- ☐ Private
- ☐ Safe
- ☐ Minimal distractions
- ☐ No interruptions
- ☐ Quiet
- ☐ Age-appropriate and somewhat familiar
- ☐ Child-sized furniture with non-thematic decorations
- ☐ Toys/interview aids
- ☐ Adequate time to acclimate
- ☐ Interview scheduled at time good for child

Psycho-social Setting

- ☐ Supportive facial expressions and relaxed body posture
- ☐ Warm, friendly intonation patterns that communicate interest in and respect for the child's views
- ☐ Patience and respect for child's silence without interruptions or further questions
- ☐ Objectivity—adopting neutral stance regarding veracity of allegations
- ☐ Acknowledging child's effort
- ☐ Being clear and explicit
- ☐ Working alliance to establish shared expectations towards a mutual goal— working together so you can understand the child's memories, thoughts, or feelings

without contaminating their accounts, even after a one-year delay. However, such support must not be tied to specific content; rather, it must be provided in a manner that is independent of the child's responses.

So as not to bias the child's responses, portray a warm demeanor, accepting of the child, while still maintaining a matter-of-fact tone about the content of the child's statements. Strive to convey that the *child's* perspective on and memory for events are what matters here. Emphasize that you will work hard to understand as much *or as little* of what the child remembers, thinks, and feels. Unlike ordinary conversations with adults, affirm that you are gathering information from the child, not judging the validity or reliability of the content of his statements. Finally, although you should avoid creating unnecessary anxiety for the child, you can communicate that the interview is a serious task and you expect the child to do his best to provide truthful and complete responses to the interviewer's questions when he can. Specific instructions to help accomplish these goals are provided in later sections of this guide.

The following checklist includes interviewer behaviors that have been found to promote an effective psycho-social environment for a child forensic interview.

Psycho-social Setting Checklist

- ✓ *Facial expression and body posture*: Convey a supportive stance toward the child by smiling, making eye contact, and maintaining a relaxed body posture.

- ✓ *Tone of voice*: Use warm, friendly intonation patterns that communicate interest in and respect for the child's views—be a listener and not an interrogator.

- ✓ *Patience*: Learn to tolerate silence and give the child time to respond without rushing in with interruptions or questions or trying to "help" the child by supplying words, thoughts, or feelings.

✓ *Objectivity*: Adopt a neutral stance regarding the veracity of any allegations—a nonjudgmental stance is key. Keep biases in check—avoid derogatory or evaluative comments (e.g., "He's bad. That was a bad thing for him to do"). Downplay your own emotional reactions—avoid expressing shock, disbelief, or frustration in response to a child's disclosure. Help the child feel he can tell what has (*or has not*) happened without upsetting or disappointing the interviewer. Under- rather than over-react.

✓ *Acknowledge children's effort*: Comment positively on the child's effort to listen carefully and pay attention, but not on the content or the accuracy of his statements (e.g., "I can see you are really working hard to listen carefully"). Beware: praise must not become selective reinforcement of responses that fit the interviewer's *a priori* beliefs.

✓ *Be clear and explicit*: Avoid ambiguity, contradiction, insincerity, and sarcasm. Young children have difficulty reading the complexity of these multi-layered communications. Your utterances should be relatively short, simple, direct, and unambiguous. Your facial expressions should match your words.

✓ *Create a working alliance*: Establish shared expectations towards a mutual goal—working together so you can understand the child's memories, thoughts, or feelings relevant to the purpose of the interview. Let the child know you need his help because you were not there and you have no special knowledge about the event.

Documentation

Interviewing a child when legal issues are pending requires thorough, conscientious documentation of both *content* and *process* that is not typically necessary with adults or in purely clinical contexts. The *content* to be documented includes the interviewer's questions as well as the child's answers as close to verbatim as possible, especially when it comes to central statements.

Interviewer's Note

In the case of the child's answers, documentation should include the child's exact wording and not a paraphrase of the child's words—especially idiosyncratic terms used by the child that reflect developmentally-appropriate reasoning. Document that the child said "White glue squirted out of his penis" rather than "Child stated suspect ejaculated." Or "He put a hot-dog balloon on his penis" rather than "Child stated he used a condom." The legal system relies on developmentally-appropriate wording as one indicia of reliability.

The *process* to be documented may include your routine practices, any necessary departures from routine practices, the reasons why the departure was necessary, and the child's nonverbal and emotional reactions at important points in the interview. You will also want to document precautions you have taken to maintain a neutral position and any evidence of a motive to fabricate false allegations, or to exaggerate, deny, or minimize genuine abuse.

Documentation During the Interview

Documentation may take the form of detailed notes or an audio or video recording. In either case, explain the reason for documentation to the child. The following is sample wording you may use:

> *What you tell me is very important. I need to remember it correctly. I am going to write it down (or audiotape/videotape what we say) so that if I forget, I can look at my notes (or listen to or watch the tape) to remember what we said.*

If you are a member of a multidisciplinary team, other team members may watch through a one-way mirror, taking notes so you can concentrate on the interview. In this case, you may want to introduce the child to the other team members in advance and tell the child they are there to take notes to help you remember later, since children can be distracted by or worried about who is behind the window.

Studies that serve as the evidence base for the DNE have videotaped interviews. If you decide to videotape the child forensic interview, you should do the following:

✓ Become familiar with the customary practices in the local legal community for recording interview results, and the policies of your agency concerning same (e.g., assent of children and consent of parents to videotape; limits on confidentiality).

✓ Obtain and maintain copies of the appropriate court orders regarding storage, destruction, duplication, access, and sanctions for misuse of videotaped materials.

✓ Provide time for the child to acclimate to the audio or video recording equipment.

Documentation After the Interview

Whether or not you videotape or audiotape, demonstrate in your notes that you were thoughtful, considered alternatives, were aware of the gravity and potentially permanent consequences of your work (e.g., out-of-home placement, termination of parental rights, adult loss of liberty), and you were alert to the potential for misuse and misinterpretations of your findings. Document any decisions you made to avoid filling multiple relationships or expanding your role: for example, choosing *not* to serve in a therapeutic role for the child or family while you are serving as a forensic interviewer, or refusing to comment on the ability of the parent to provide the right care for the child because your work has been focused on interviewing the child, not evaluating the parent. A thorough documentation of content and process ensures accountability and will make it much more difficult for an attorney in cross-examination to successfully indict your credibility, and therefore undermine the child's testimony.

Conclusion

In conclusion, your goal is to create a developmentally sensitive setting to facilitate the child's cooperation, motivation, and optimal performance. Your objective in documenting the content of the interview is to provide as complete, accurate, and faithful a recording of what was said and what occurred during the interview as possible. Your aim in documenting the process of the interview is to demonstrate your objectivity and the forensic justifiability of your work.

Chapter 4 *Beginning the Interview: Introductions, Creating a Template, and Developing Rapport*

Materials Needed

- Crayons/markers and blank paper (optional)
- Simple stencils (optional)

Outline

- Introduce your role
- Explain the interview mechanics, agenda and purpose, and the child's role
- Break the ice and build rapport
- Use initial conversation to create a template for later questioning

Introduction

Fundamental to DNE are practices designed to bridge the gap between the demands of the interview task and the child's developmental limitations. Forensic interviews require a level of honesty, openness, and effort from children that is rare in their interactions with strangers. From the start, DNE procedures acknowledge that the child may be unfamiliar with you, your purpose, and the implicit requirements of the forensic context. Thoughtful introductions, explicit explanations, precautions, modeling, and practice are designed to bridge the gap.

Early conversation demonstrates that rules for interaction in a forensic setting are different from those in ordinary conversation. Early explanations address limitations in children's knowledge of the legal system, and their failure to appreciate the larger implications and consequences of their behaviors or statements in the interview. Efforts to develop rapport and build trust are designed to demonstrate that you will respect the child's opinions, perceptions, and coping strategies; that you are motivated to do your best to understand fully, not manipulate, his perceptions and responses; that you are willing to accept however much or little information he wants to offer; and that you will be honest with him in return.

Introduction of Your Role

You should begin by telling the child your name and defining your role (see Table 4.1 for sample ways to define the interviewer's role).

Table 4.1 Sample Ways to Introduce Your Role

Mental Health Professional

■ You can tell the child your job is to help children and families with problems. Although you are indicating that problems may be the topic of discussion, you are allowing the child to choose the problem area to be talked about.

Protective services worker or law enforcement officer

■ You can inform the child your job is to help children and families stay safe and healthy, and this suggests that violations of safety are legitimate topics for discussion.

■ Later, you can ask the child: "What makes you feel safe? What makes you feel not safe?" and the questions will make sense in the context of your job. It can lead to a disclosure of forensically relevant information without your using leading techniques.

In custody cases

■ You can tell the child your job is to help the judge make the best plan for the child's entire family.

■ Then, you can begin your substantive questioning with this question: "Is there something you think I should know or tell the judge?" Children will understand the purpose of this non-leading question and it may reduce the likelihood that more leading questions will be necessary.

Depending on your discipline and purpose, with young children you may say your job is one or more of the following:

- To keep children and families safe

- To help children and families solve problems

- To allow important decisions to be made regarding the best plan for the child's family

Explanation of the Mechanics of the Interview, Its Agenda and Purpose, and the Child's Role

Children have little reason to cooperate with unfamiliar adults for unknown purposes. They need to understand your intentions and what will happen during the time they spend with you. This demystifies the situation and helps children provide the most complete statements in their own words with the least prompting. To maximize their effort and cooperation, outline what will happen in simple, observable terms, including where caretakers will be waiting and what the child is expected to do. The following is sample language you may use:

> *We will be sitting at this table and talking in this room. We will be here about half an hour (as long as one television program). Your mom will be waiting in the waiting room until we are finished. After we get to know each other a little bit better, I may ask you some questions about what you have seen or heard or felt. Your job is to tell me your answers as best you can. Then you can ask me some questions, too. When we are done, I will walk you back to your mom.*

Once the mechanics and purpose of the interview have been explained, the child can focus on the interview rather than worry about unrealistic, imagined possibilities.

Refer to Table 4.2 for a checklist of introductions and explanations prior to the core interview.

Table 4.2 Checklist for Introductions and Explanations

- Outline what will happen in the interview.

- Introduce yourself by defining your role.

- Explain the child's role as a witness.

- Describe the mechanics and purpose of the interview.

- Discuss limits on confidentiality—optional.

- Outline the information-gathering and decision-making aspects of the legal process briefly in an age-appropriate fashion to dispel unrealistic expectations and fears (as discussed in Chapter 5).

- Provide explanations of how the interview differs from everyday conversation (as discussed in Chapter 5).

Breaking the Ice and Building Rapport

There is no set list of topics to discuss during rapport development; however, in an opening gambit, avoid anxiety-provoking, pointed, personal questions, and facts of the case. From the start, it is important to remember that, during the process of establishing rapport, you are establishing a template for the interactions to follow.

You can start by indicating that you want to get to know the child better by saying something general, such as the following:

- "I'd like to get to know you better. Tell me about something important to you."

- "That sounds interesting; tell me more. What happened next?"

You can also repeat what the child has said with a rising intonation to invite the child to expand on her statement. Then follow-up with simple, open-ended prompts and questions that require multi-word responses to help children practice elaborating in their own words.

In these initial interactions, strive to convey understanding for the child's perspective without suggestion or bias. By listening attentively and limiting comments to repetitions of a child's thoughts or feelings, you demonstrate you have heard the child's perception of the situation without agreeing or validating it as true. By asking for elaboration with minimal prompts (e.g., "What happened next?" "You said X happened, tell me more."), you demonstrate genuine interest without a hidden agenda and model that the child is expected to do more of the talking than the interviewer.

The amount of time devoted to rapport development will vary with the child's attention span, temperament, and the facts of the case, but it need not be too long. In our studies, initial efforts to establish rapport vary from two to ten minutes. A few rapport-building activities are suggested below. In addition, the pre-interview activities (described in Chapters 6 and 7) are designed to engage children in a working alliance towards the goals of optimal communication and memory performance. In our experience, children find these activities engaging and interesting, and rapport continues to develop over the course of these activities. Efforts to maintain rapport and deepen trust should be continued as necessary throughout the interview.

Sample Activities

Following are some sample activities you may use for initiating conversations:

- For children of all ages, the interviewer can ask about activities that are important to the child (e.g., sports, arts) or ask the child to describe the story of a favorite book, movie, or television episode. (e.g., "What's your favorite TV show? Tell me what happened in one of the stories."). This demonstrates your desire to learn more about the child from the child's perspective, and establishes your role as a listener, with no hidden agenda, rather than an interrogator.

- For the very young child, the interviewer can comment on the room and then ask the child to describe the room (e.g., "Let's talk together. Tell me about this room we are sitting in. What do you see/notice?"). Take turns noticing various aspects of the room. This is a shared activity that helps establish a working alliance—the mutuality of the interview ahead—and the turn-taking format of the interview. It allows the child to acclimate to the surroundings. It also produces a sample of the child's language that you can use later to guide your own language.

- For quiet, shy children with limited verbal output, you might start with crayons and paper. Trace your hand (or a simple stencil) and then ask the child to do the same with his hand (or stencil). Again, this is an activity that sets up an expectation for turn-taking and a mutual interaction.

Using Initial Conversation to Create a Template for Later Questioning

Early conversation is a pivotal part of the DNE approach. It establishes the template for the rest of the interview. From the start, initial conversation should send the message that the child is to provide as much detail as possible on his own, with minimal prompting from the interviewer. Therefore, use open-ended questions that require multi-word responses to develop rapport and avoid questions that require *yes* or *no* responses.

Why is it so important to establish the interview template at the very beginning, especially with children younger than eight years of age? From conversations with parents or caretakers, children learn to expect that adults will "scaffold" language learning and carry the burden of conversation by expanding children's answers; extending the meaning of their responses; taking responsibility for corrections, clarification, and repairs; providing extra feedback; and asking questions to which adults already know the answers. During rapport development in the DNE, children learn that the rules of interaction in the forensic context are different.

In addition, initial conversation provides a sample of the child's language that you can use to gauge how to simplify your own language during the substantive part of the interview. If you notice a child uses short sentences and one- to two-syllable words, then later you can take care to avoid lengthy, grammatically complex utterances containing three- to four-syllable words.

In the DNE, give the child at least 5–10 seconds to answer any questions or expand on his own narratives. Children, especially young children, often need time to process the syntax and cognitive demands of an adult's question and to formulate answers. You want to show that you can tolerate silence and momentary lapses in the child's motivation, memory, or language abilities without rushing in with unsolicited clarifications of the original question or additional questions. Impatience can be perceived as your disappointment or the child's "failure." Tolerating the silence emphasizes that there are no right or wrong answers, and that the child's report, not the adult's agenda, is primary.

Overcoming Anxiety or Reluctance

If the child expresses anxiety or appears angry or upset, refrain from downplaying or devaluing the significance of her feelings. Avoid comments such as, "Don't worry," "Don't feel nervous," or "Don't be upset/ angry." Instead, ask if there is anything you can do to make it easier for the child to feel comfortable. Showing that you are trying to understand her perspective requires developmental sensitivity.

Coping with Separation Anxiety in Young Children

Before meeting, give caretakers instructions to inform the child of your name and that you will expect the child to accompany you to your office. Also have caretakers reassure the child that he will be safe with you and will not experience any unpredictable behaviors or activities—the two of you will be talking and maybe drawing together, but not much else.

Upon meeting, greet the child by name with eye contact, warmth, and acceptance. Your first inclination may be to address the adult accompanying the child. However, at this moment you are largely unaware of the complex dynamics between the child and this adult. Given the adversarial context of the legal system, unthinking comments by you to the adult can be construed by the child as taking sides. Your trustworthiness is a commodity you do not want to squander.

Let the child know where significant others are waiting. If necessary, consider allowing the child to check on them periodically during the interview. You can comment on the child's fears and reassure him about his own and his caretakers' safety (e.g., "I wonder if you are worried that your mom might not be here when we come out. Mrs. M, will you please stay right here in this chair while we talk in the other room so Jamal does not need to worry about you?").

If the child refuses to leave the caretaker's side, consider inviting the caretaker to join the beginning of the interview process. Phase I of the interview can be carried out with caretakers present. As mentioned above, you should ask caretakers to sit behind the child during Phase I and to leave when you begin Phase II. You can instruct caretakers to refrain from helping children answer questions and to redirect children back to you.

Coping with Reluctance in Older Children[1]

Often, there are very good reasons why a child should think twice about sharing details about private family matters, such as abuse or neglect, with relative strangers (Lyon, 2007; Lyon, Ahern, Malloy, & Quas, 2010).

✓ **Accept and understand rather than challenge or minimize a child's reluctance.** Acknowledge that people usually have good reasons for doing what they do. State that you think the child may have a good reason for his reluctance to talk with you. Ask what that reason might be. Sample language follows:

Most people have good reasons for what they do. You probably have a good reason for why you would rather not be here/rather not be talking to me today. Can you help me understand what your reasons might be?

Here is an example of a dialogue between an interviewer and child:

INTERVIEWER: "Maybe you are right, you shouldn't be here. Can you help me understand the reasons why you don't want to be here?"

CHILD: "I've already talked with three other people about it and nothing has changed. Nothing will change if I talk to you."

INTERVIEWER: "What do you want to change?"

CHILD: "I want my dad to stop drinking."

In this case, asking the boy what he wanted to change in a non-leading open-ended fashion became the first step in a conversation about his stepfather's alcoholism and violence towards the mother and younger brother.

✓ **Empathize with ambivalence.** Be sensitive to ambivalent feelings about discussing private family matters with relative strangers, especially when parents are suspected perpetrators of abuse or neglect. Instead, normalize ambivalence by appealing to the idea that everyone has conflicting feelings at times; that is, they find themselves in situations where a part of them wants to do something and another part does not. Comments along the following lines can be useful to open up a discussion:

Maybe a part of you wants to talk about what's happening in your life or your family—maybe that part wants something to change. But another part of you wants to keep it inside or to remain silent.

✓ **Explore, rather than avoid, a genuine discussion of the downsides of self-disclosure.** Here is an example of such an exploration:

INTERVIEWER: "What might happen if you told me the things you think you should keep quiet about?"

CHILD: "My grandpa will be furious, my mom will fall apart, and I will get taken away."

INTERVIEWER: "Why do you think those things would happen?"

CHILD: "My uncle will be in trouble. I'm not supposed to talk about the drugs."

✓ **Make a list of pros and cons of participating.** Some of the cognitive advances in older children can actually aid in building rapport, enabling them to make a list of the pros and cons of cooperating, see problems from different angles, and adopt multiple viewpoints.

For example, if an older child walks in, puts his hood over his head, and turns his back to you, you can comment that he would rather not be here or seems to want to be somewhere else. Suggest that he probably has good reasons for not wanting to talk to you. Together you might create a list of Reasons Not to Talk ("This stuff is embarrassing." and "I've already told my social worker.") and Reasons to Talk ("I guess that will make this time easier."). This activity engages the child at the same time as it respects his freedom to choose not to cooperate.

✓ **Convey respect for older children's opinion and autonomy.**
Older children often feel controlled, misunderstood, and intruded upon. Authoritarian approaches or techniques designed to reduce freedom of choice can backfire. Avoid a power struggle. Rather, find ways the child can save face and avoid embarrassment; help him feel empowered to be honest and open, even if he is angry.

For example, if an older child announces, "I am only here because the judge is making me be here, but you can't make me talk to you," you may agree that he is in control of whether he talks or not, and then ask, "Why does the judge think it is a good idea for you to talk to me?" This question will help the child distance himself from his own perspective and take that of the judge. In one case, the child answered, "He wants to know what happened to my little brother." The interviewer inquired, "Why does the judge need to know?" The child took the judge's viewpoint and replied, "He has to figure out if we can go back to my mom's house. My mom has problems. She has bad friends who give her drugs and she forgets things...."

Conclusion

From the start of the DNE interview, your goal is to bridge the gap between the child's limitations in knowledge and experience and the requirements of the unfamiliar forensic context. Your aims in this preliminary phase are: (a) to provide clear introductions and explicit explanations of your role, the child's role, and the mechanics and purpose of the interview in a developmentally sensitive manner; (b) to set up a template for future discourse that establishes you as a listener, not an interrogator, and the child as a provider of as much detail as possible in his own words with minimal prompting; (c) to develop rapport and a relationship that facilitates trust and honesty so you can understand what is important to the child; and (d) to address anxieties and resistances that interfere with creating a working alliance towards the goals of the interview.

Chapter 5

Demystifying the Legal Process and the Interview

Materials Needed

None

Outline

- Demystify the legal process
- Employ toolkit of interview pointers and explanations as appropriate

Introduction

Imagine playing football when you don't know the rules, or navigating a foreign culture without a guide, itinerary, or a facility for the language. This is a young child's predicament when confronted with the unique demands of a forensic context. Nevertheless, the interviewer can circumvent, in part, children's confusion, misperception, and unrealistic fears by demystifying the legal process and providing them with clear and explicit instructions on the "rules" of the interview.

Demystifying the Legal Process

While children may have some knowledge of the legal system (often derived from television), they have gaps and distortions that can lead to incomplete reports and unrealistic fears. For example, our research has shown that some children fear they may go to jail as a result of making a mistake in a forensic interview. This fear could lead to more "I don't know" responses from the child (Saywitz, 1989).

A child's fears will automatically be addressed in the process of educating her about her role as a witness and the likely route a case will take through the system. However, it is important to educate children about the legal process in a manner that is both relevant to the specific case and appropriate for the child's age. Sample comments from our research follow (Nathanson & Saywitz, 2003). However, if an interviewer has reason to believe it is unwise or unnecessary to discuss such issues prior to a particular interview, such discussions are not mandatory.

Four- to Six-Year-Olds

For four- to six-year-olds in a criminal investigation:

- Explain the investigative phase as the information-gathering phase: "First, we find out as much information as we can. We talk to you. We may ask other people questions, too."

- Describe the flow of information from interviewer to decision-makers, referring back to your explanation of your role in the process: "Then we tell the information (what we have learned) to the people who have to make decisions about solving the problem/keeping children and families safe/making the best decision for your family."

Seven- to Twelve-Year-Olds

For seven- to twelve-year-olds in a criminal investigation, we have used an analogy in our research that likens an investigation to a classroom altercation while the teacher is out of the room. To help provide an explanation that improves children's comprehension of the process, sample discussion points follow:

- When the teacher returns, one child accuses another of misbehavior. The teacher must decide if any rules were broken.

She questions both children involved and any bystanders (e.g., students who saw what happened). If there is enough information to suggest broken rules, she passes this along to the principal. Then the principal decides if something should be done or someone should be punished.

- Similarly, the interviewer gathers information from witnesses (like the child) to decide if any laws were broken (or if anyone needs protection). If there is enough reason to think a law was broken (or action should be taken), then the information is passed along (to the social worker, police officer, district attorney, or judge) for further decision-making.

Toolkit of Interview Pointers

The following list should be viewed as a "toolkit" of explanations that demonstrate how interactions in the forensic interview differ from everyday conversations. They are designed to orient children to some of the unique task demands of the forensic context and have been tested in empirical studies. Much as a carpenter brings a complete bag of tools to each job, but actually uses only the tools required for the specific job he is working on, depending on the individual and unique needs of the specific job, you should consider the following list as your toolkit of interview pointers. It is not a litany of mandatory instructions given to each child indiscriminately. For young children below seven to nine years of age, a boring recitation of the entire list could be cognitively overwhelming and socially off-putting. Your toolkit consists of a variety of interview pointers, some of which you will use, and some of which you won't use, depending on the child's cognitive and attentional resources and motivation, as well as the circumstances of the case and interview.

Individual pointers can be embedded in your introductions of your role and the child's role and interview objectives, or used at any time throughout the interview: at the beginning and/or later in the interview, for example, as necessary to redirect children's attention or re-engage them in the process. Thus, it is not necessary to give every child every one of the following interview pointers prior to questioning; doing so could overwhelm young children's cognitive processing. The only pointer given to all the children in each of the narrative elaboration studies is a variation of the first one—the instruction to encourage completeness and accuracy with minimal prompting.

Encouraging Complete, Accurate, Detailed Answers

As gathering a complete and accurate account is of utmost importance, the DNE includes encouraging children to give detailed answers, as in the following sample dialogues:

- *I am going to ask you some questions. There are two important things to know when you answer. First, try to tell as much as you can remember, even the little things that you might not think are important. Number two, when you tell me about something that happened, tell only what really happened. Don't guess or make anything up. Only tell what you remember.* [OR]

- *Tell me what happened from the beginning, to the middle, to the end. Sometimes people don't tell about the little things because they think that little things are not important. Tell me everything you remember, even the little things that you think are not very important. The more you can tell me about what happened, the more I will understand what happened. Please remember I was not there when it happened.*

Instructing Children to Tell the Truth

Like most interview protocols, the DNE informs children of their obligation to tell the truth in the forensic interview. You may want to use the following language:

While we are talking together today, it is important to tell the truth. Only tell what really happened. Don't make anything up. Don't guess.

Instructing Children that You Cannot Help Them Answer the Questions

As noted earlier, children are accustomed to interacting with parents and teachers who often know the answers to their questions. Thus, children can benefit from being told explicitly that you will rely on the child's report to fully understand what happened. For example:

I was not there. I could not know what happened. I will not be able to help you answer the questions. I am interested in learning what you think, what you remember, and what you feel. That is what's important.

Instructing Children to Pay Attention

Young children have not developed the level of self-control seen in school-age children who can sit in their seat and raise their hands when they want to speak. Therefore, younger children often need to be redirected to the task at hand throughout the interview, using the following instructions:

- *Listen carefully.*

- *Pay attention. Look at me.*

- *Think about your answers.*

- *Take your time. Don't hurry.*

Warning Children That Some Questions Might Be Hard to Understand

When settings are unfamiliar and tasks are complex and verbal—such as in forensic interviews—young children often have difficulty recognizing whether or not they understand an adult's questions, and they are unlikely to ask for clarification. The following sample language is useful to help children identify questions beyond their understanding and ask for rephrasing:

Sometimes I might ask a question that you don't understand. Some questions might be easy to understand but some might be hard to understand. If I ask a question you don't understand, tell me. I will ask it again using words you do understand. You can say, "I don't

understand. I don't get it." Or say, *"Tell me in new/different words."*
[Children under seven may not fully understand the meaning of
the word "different," in which case you can use the term "new" as
an alternative.]

Promoting Motivation and Effort

As the interview may be a challenging task for a child, there may be
instances when you want to use motivational language.

- *Do your best.*

- *Try your hardest.*

Permission to Say "I Don't Know" and Correct Interviewer Mistakes

To clarify task demands and interviewer expectations, children can be told
that they are not required to respond to every question with a substantive
answer; instead, they can admit lack of knowledge or memory. They can
correct the interviewer if she puts her guess into a question inadvertently
or makes a mistake. You may say something like the following:

- *Some questions might be easy, but some might be hard. I don't expect
  you to know the answer to every question or to remember everything.
  Just tell what you do remember; tell me the answer if you know the
  answer.*

- *It is also important for you to tell me when you don't know the answer.
  Say, "I don't know." Or "I don't remember." But if you know the
  answer, tell the answer.*

- *Sometimes when grownups ask children questions, a grownup might
  put her guess about what happened into a question. She may make a
  mistake. It is important for you to tell me if I make a mistake. I want
  you to correct me. Tell me I made a mistake. Say "No, that's wrong,"
  if I say something that is wrong.*

- *And, if you just don't know the answer, or if you don't remember, tell
  me. But if you know the answer, tell me the answer.*

Interviewer's Note

Place the emphasis on telling the answer if the child knows it. End with this admonition.

Conclusion

This chapter offers suggestions for demystifying the legal process and explaining the forensic context to children in a developmentally sensitive fashion. Also, it provides a toolkit of interview pointers that have been used in our studies and are designed to promote completeness and accuracy, motivation, attention, honesty, and clear communication. Again, these instructions are not intended to be a lecture that will overwhelm a child's information-processing capabilities. Instead, they can be used individually, at the interviewer's discretion. The only one used in every study of the DNE is the instruction regarding completeness and accuracy. Table 5.1 presents a sample script of instructions provided to a nine-year-old boy.

Table 5.1 Case Example: Sample Script of Pointers Given to Nine-Year-Old Boy

- "Thank you for coming. Today when we talk together I am going to ask you some questions. It is very important that you—
  - Listen carefully and pay attention.
  - Take your time. If you need to think about an answer, I can wait."

- "Some of the questions might be easy to understand, and some might be hard to understand. If I ask a question you do not understand, tell me. You can say "I don't get it," or "I don't understand," and I will ask it again with different words."

- "When you answer, try your best to tell me as much as you can without guessing, even the little things. Sometimes people don't tell the little things. They think that little things are not important. Today, tell me everything, even the little things you think are not important."

- "I will not be able to help you answer the questions. If you think I already know something, please tell me in your own words anyway. It is important for me to understand how you see things and what you remember."

- "Today, it is important to tell the truth—only tell what really happened. Don't make something up. Don't guess. If you don't know the answer, tell me you don't know. But if you know the answer, tell the answer."

Chapter 6   *Before the Core Interview: Teaching the Narrative Elaboration Strategy*

Materials Needed

- Reminder cards (drawings in Appendices A and B can be photocopied and cut into individual cards)

- Picture storybook for preschoolers (optional)

Outline

- Provide a rationale for using new memory strategy

- Introduce the event categories on reminder cards

- Practice with reminder cards, model giving more details, and provide feedback

- Summarize what the child has learned

Introduction

During the preliminary phase, interviewers will be assessing whether or not a particular child will benefit from some of the optional components of the DNE. Again, the DNE is not a rigid protocol, but an overall template with a toolkit of optional techniques to be employed at the interviewer's discretion. In this guide we provide two options for eliciting a child's elaborated narrative during the core interview—one using visual cues and one using verbal cues. The focus of the present chapter is the visual-cue option for narrative elaboration, which is the original and most well-researched option. Alternatively, you can use the basic interview template without this optional technique by proceeding to Chapter 8 and following instructions for using the verbal cues to help children elaborate on their initial narratives.

The visual-cue option requires a pre-interview activity in which the child is taught how to organize retrieval efforts around four categories of forensically relevant information, prior to the core interview. Interviewers demonstrate the kinds and levels of detail the interviewer expects the child will learn to report independently. Each category is depicted by a generic line drawing on a reminder card. The drawings can be found in Appendices A and B, photocopied, and cut out as individual cards. As you will see from the sample script that follows, a few variations of this technique are provided. This is because each time the NE technique was tested, researchers in various laboratories, in several countries, and with diverse populations have used slightly different versions (refer to Chapter 2). The good news is that all of these variations have been found to be beneficial to children and superior to standard protocols, suggesting that the effect is robust, so you have the flexibility to determine which variation is best suited to a given case.

Deciding When to Use Visual Cues and When to Use Verbal Cues to Aid Narrative Elaboration

When considering whether to use the visual-cues (reminder cards) or verbal-cues option, consider the following:

- The NE procedure with visual cues (reminder cards) has been shown to be beneficial for children of all ages in the three- to 12-year-old age range, and for children who are often considered more difficult to interview because they are from disadvantaged backgrounds, or have lower IQ scores, limited vocabularies, and/ or learning disabilities. In addition, we find that in the unfamiliar, verbally complex interview context, some children, regardless of age, appear confused, minimally responsive, distracted, or inattentive. For these children, the external visual cues may help them focus and sustain their attention and clarify task demands (as described in Chapter 2).

- The visual-cue option, however, does require a brief explanation and practice with the reminder cards prior to beginning the core interview (as outlined in this chapter). Children tend to find this pre-interview activity both engaging and interesting. However, when interviewers do not have the extra time, or when children do not have the attentional resources, interviewers can conduct a purely verbal interview that requires no practice or reminder cards.

- The verbal-cue option consists of a short set of verbal prompts about the same four categories of information inserted into the core interview before you begin your specific follow-up questions (as described in Chapter 8).

- The verbal-cue option may provide comparable results for many children, especially for typically developing elementary school–aged children (Brown & Pipe, 2003b). While no researchers have yet compared the two options with preschoolers, there is evidence that the verbal-cue option should be beneficial to younger children, based on studies using somewhat similar verbal prompts with preschoolers (Elischberger & Roebers, 2001; Kulkofsky, 2010; Poole & Lindsay, 1995).[1] Further research is needed to understand the effects of the verbal-cue option with fictitious events, and the benefits of the verbal-cue options with children who have learning disabilities, or children from disadvantaged backgrounds.

Start by Providing a Rationale for Using Reminder Cards

Studies show that children benefit from being given a rationale for learning new retrieval strategies. Hence, we start by impressing on children the value of learning new ways to help them remember better and how to identify difficult situations that call for strategy usage.

Preschoolers and Delayed, Inattentive, or Confused Children

Children three to six years old, or who may be delayed or confused, need a simplified rationale for the use of reminder cards.

Option A

- Begin with the following language: *I am going to teach you a special way to remember a lot.*

- Then proceed to introducing the reminder cards.

Option B

- Ask the child to draw something freehand (e.g., a circle or animal) and then to draw it using a stencil (e.g., lid of a jar or animal stencil).

- Ask which one makes a better circle/picture. Children invariably select the lid/stencil.

- Explain that *sometimes you can do things better if you do something extra to help yourself do it better, like using the lid/stencil.*

Proceed to introducing the reminder cards as another way to help themselves do things better.

Rationale for Older Children

For older children in elementary school, we have used a rationale that demonstrates the value of using a specific memory strategy, such as the following:

Sometimes remembering is easy, but sometimes it is hard.

For example, if a grownup sends you to the store and has a lot of things for you to buy, you can try to remember all the things in your head. But if there are a lot of things, you might forget some. What could you do to help yourself remember better? What might be a better way to help you remember? [Pause to allow the child to generate ideas, such as making a list, writing things down.]

Right, a better way to remember everything might be to write things down, make a list. You can look at the list as you go, that way you won't forget anything.

So you see, there are better and worse ways to remember things. Today I'm going to teach you a better way to remember things when you have to tell someone about things that happened. [Proceed to introducing reminder cards]

Introducing the Event Categories

Next, we introduce children to the notion that they can organize their elaboration around four parts of what happened (i.e., event categories):

- *Participants*: The People Card (Who was there)

- *Settings*: The Places Card (Where it happened)

- *Actions*: The What Happened Card (What happened; What people did)

- *Conversations/Affective States*: The Talking/Feeling Card (What people said and how they felt)

There are two versions of the reminder cards: one set for school-age children (in Appendix A) and one for preschoolers (in Appendix B).

For Children of All Ages

1. Introduce the event categories by placing the stack of reminder cards before the child and saying,

   - *A good way to tell about things that happen to you is to use these reminder cards. These four cards remind you of all the things/parts to tell when you talk about things that happened to you.*

2. Hold up each card individually in turn and say,

   - *This is the People Card; it reminds you to tell who was there and how the people looked.*
   - *This is the Places Card; it reminds you to tell where it was and how the place looked.*

- *This is the What Happened Card; it reminds you to tell everything about what happened and what people did.*
- *This is the Talking/Feeling Card; it reminds you to tell about what people said and how they felt.*

For Very Young Children

If you are concerned that a very young child will not understand the representational nature of the cards, you can show the child a line drawing of a red and a green traffic light before you introduce the reminder cards. Ask the child:

What do these lights tell you to do? [Pause to allow child to answer]

Yes, that's right, the red light tells you to stop. The green light tells you to go.

Here I have four reminder cards. These cards tell you what to do, too. They tell you how to say all you remember, even the little things. Each card shows a part of what happened.

Practice with Reminder Cards, Modeling Detail and Providing Feedback

Once all the cards have been introduced, do a practice run, beginning with the following:

Let's learn how to use them now. If you were going to tell someone/your mom about your meeting with me so far, what would you tell them/ your mom?

This practice task requires the child to recall an easily remembered, live event that the interviewer can verify in order to provide corrective feedback. It is appropriate for all children between four and 12 years of age.

Alternative Practice Task for Preschoolers

If you deem it appropriate, you have the option of using an alternative practice task with young children, especially those who are reticent or easily distracted and have difficulty paying attention to purely verbal material. As an alternative, you can read a short age-appropriate picture book and ask the child to retell the story while looking at the pictures. As in the practice task of recalling a live event (i.e., what you and the child have done together thus far), the interviewer can correct the child because the book is present during the retelling. Both practice tasks have been beneficial in NE research studies, as described in Chapter 2.

Guidelines for Practice Task

The following steps are a guideline for practicing with the reminder cards on the mock recall task. Modeling demonstrates the kinds of information and degree of detail that the task requires. Corrective feedback will demonstrate how to elaborate on initial narratives without guessing or making up details.

1. Ask the child to recall what you and he have done together thus far in the interview (or recall a picture-book story if you chose this option for a preschooler). Allow the child to respond to your invitation to tell about the interview thus far without interruption (or to provide recall of the story).

2. When the child appears to be finished, ask, "Is that all?" or "Anything else?" and wait for the child's response. (Use a matter-of-fact tone of voice, not one that implies the child's answer is insufficient. The goal is only to provide another opportunity for reporting.) Usually children describe the actions that occurred but do not spontaneously describe the participants, conversations, feeling states, or locations in any detail.

3. After the child is finished responding, introduce a reminder card. For example:

    Good. Now, let's use the reminder cards to tell more about what happened. This is the People Card; it reminds you to tell about all the people who were there, what their names were, and how each person looked. If you were going to tell someone all about our time together, you would tell them about the people you met—like me—what I look like, my name, and what I am wearing. What would you tell them about me?

4. Allow the child to respond without interruption. When the child indicates she is finished, say

   Good job, you told a lot about me. There might be even more things you could tell if you remembered them.

5. Model telling a few additional details the child could mention if they were recalled, such as your name; gender; skin color; hair color, length, and texture; body size; clothing color and style; and other distinguishing characteristics. Typically, we demonstrate about three details with each card, as in the following example: "You could also tell that my name is Joan, that I have long black hair, or I wear glasses."

6. Also, practice praising the child's effort and not the content (e.g., "I appreciate how hard you are working; Thanks for trying your best and listening carefully"); providing corrective feedback if the child says anything obviously inaccurate; and reminding the child to tell only what she really knows and remembers. When children comment that they cannot remember something (e.g., "There was another guy, but I can't remember his name") praise the child for only telling what he remembers.

7. Repeat this same procedure with each of the remaining reminder cards, reviewing what the card is used for, allowing the child to practice with the card, providing the child with feedback, and modeling telling two or three additional details.

Again, it is worth highlighting that the goal is not to encourage blind enumeration of endless detail. Interviewers want to provide just enough modeling so children get the idea that the task involves independent provision of details related to the four categories of event information and enough corrective feedback that children understand they are not to move beyond what they can actually recall. A sample script of a child learning to use the reminder cards is provided in Appendix C.

Elaborating Affective States

For the Talking/Feeling Card, when children report a participant's feeling state, remind the child to describe the behaviors she observed that indicated any feeling states (e.g., "You said he was mad. What makes you think he was mad?" "What did he do to let you know he was mad?" "What did he say to make you think he was mad?").

To help children practice elaborating on affective states, we have done the following in some of our studies: During the introductions and the rapport-development phase, the interviewer looks for a lost pen and comments that it makes him sad that it is lost because he received it as a birthday gift and it was his favorite one. Later, in the practice with the Feeling Card, the interviewer can ask the child how the interviewer was feeling about losing his pen and model that the child could tell he was sad when he lost it and happy when he found it. For example:

INTERVIEWER: How do you think I was feeling when I lost my pen?

CHILD: Sad.

INTERVIEWER: What makes you think I was sad?

CHILD: You said it was your favorite. You said you were sad if you lost it.

INTERVIEWER: Good job telling me what we said. If you remember, you could tell that I was happy when I found it. Do you think I was happy?

CHILD: Yes.

INTERVIEWER: What made you think so?

CHILD: You smiled. You said you were happy.

Additional Practice Tasks if Deemed Necessary

Studies suggest that most children need to practice only once with the cards to benefit. Occasionally, a second practice is deemed helpful to a child. In this case, children practice retelling what they did that morning from the time they got up until the time they arrived at the interview, using the reminder cards. A transcript of an interview with a preschooler using the latter scenario appears in Appendix D.

Summarizing What the Child Has Learned

At the end of the practice, summarizing back to the child what she has learned helps cement the new skills. You may want to use the following language while showing the child each of the cards for review:

Nice job!! You used the cards and you remembered a lot. You learned you can remember things and tell about them better when you use these cards. [Hold up the participants card.] *The People Card reminds you to tell who was there and how each person looked;* [hold up settings card] *the Places Card reminds you to tell where it was and how the place looked;* [hold up action card] *the What Happened Card reminds you to tell what happened, what people did;* [hold up conversation/affective states card] *and the Talking/Feeling Card reminds you to tell what people said and how they felt. Also, you learned to tell as much as you can remember, even the little things, but not to guess.*

Conclusion

This chapter describes a brief procedure (NE) conducted at the end of the preliminary phase that teaches children how to elaborate on their reports in their own words by demonstrating the kind of information and the level of detail expected in the forensic context. The NE procedure involves (a) providing children with a rationale for learning a new strategy, (b) practicing the strategy on one mock recall task, and (c) then summarizing what the child has learned. The strategy involves elaborating on the Participants, Setting, Actions, and Conversations/Affective States. Later, when conducting the core interview, the visual cues (reminder cards) can be used again to cue children to use the new strategy during the core interview.

Chapter 7

Before the Core Interview: Optional Methods for Improving Communication and Resisting Suggestion

Materials Needed

- Thinking Cards (optional)

Outline

- Employ DNE strategies for promoting communication as appropriate
- Employ DNE strategies for resisting suggestion as appropriate

Introduction

In this chapter, we describe two optional strategies that can be used to supplement the principal DNE when the interviewer deems them to be useful. They are designed to improve accuracy of children's memory reports by reducing miscommunication and acquiescence to misleading questions. If interviewers choose not to use these optional techniques, they can proceed to the core interview as described in Chapter 8.

As discussed in Chapter 2, researchers find that when children practice detecting incomprehensible questions and requesting a simpler rephrase from the interviewer, their answers to substantive follow-up questions improve dramatically (Peters & Nunez, 1999; Saywitz et al., 1999). Hence, the procedure for teaching children this strategy is described below. In addition, researchers find that making school-age children aware of the fact that interviewers may inadvertently put their guess into a question, and that children do not have to answer every question substantively, but rather have the option to say "I don't know, I don't remember" or to correct the interviewer, reduces children's acquiescence to misleading questions (Krackow & Lynn, 2009; Saywitz & Moan-Hardie, 1994). The procedure for increasing children's awareness of these options is described below as well.

Interviewers are urged to observe the child during the initial introductions, explanations, and rapport-building to judge whether to employ these optional DNE components. Sometimes you will want to forgo these optional techniques because the child appears engaged, talkative, forthcoming, and ready to proceed to the core interview without further ado. In other cases, you may want to forgo these optional techniques because time is of the essence or you are concerned that a child will be less productive overall if too much time is spent in the beginning before initiating the core interview.

At other times, however, you might notice that a younger child appears inattentive, reticent, and confused, or that a child seems unaware of the context and not particularly talkative or engaged, avoiding eye contact. You may decide that such a child could benefit from the increased time to develop rapport while engaging in one or two optional goal-directed activities that structure the time and focus the child's attention on the task at hand. Typically, children find the activities engaging and interesting. We find these activities serve to establish the interactive, turn-taking format of the interview and engage the child in a working alliance toward interview goals—not to mention the added benefit of improving the reliability and completeness of the child's memory report and preventing communication breakdowns and misinterpretations later.

Promoting Communication: Strategies for Comprehension Monitoring and Asking for Rephrase

Providing a Rationale for Admitting Lack of Comprehension

The following dialogue intentionally introduces an incomprehensible question (through coughing and nonsense words that obscure intelligibility) to help the child recognize the need for admitting lack of comprehension.

Sometimes grownups ask questions that are hard to understand. For example, if a grownup asked you, "How much [coughing] did you snurkel at bumbleding?" would you understand that?

[Wait for child to answer.]

So if you don't understand a question, you can tell the grownup you do not understand. Say, "I don't get it. What do you mean?" or "I don't understand your question." When children do this, grownups are able to ask the question using words the children do understand, and then nobody gets confused.

When you do not understand my question, ask me to say it in new words.

For Preschoolers, add: *You can put your hand out like a policeman does to stop traffic to show me you want me to stop* [demonstrate holding out your arm with your hand flexed as if stopping something].

Practice Detecting Incomprehensible Questions and Asking for a Rephrase

Once the child has a grasp of the rationale for admitting lack of comprehension, move on to actual practice; you may want to use language such as the following:

Okay, let's try it now. I am going to ask you some questions about our time together today. Remember if you do not understand a question I ask you, don't answer it. Instead [for younger children you can add: *put your hand out like a police officer to stop me*], *say "I don't get it. What do you mean?" or "I don't understand your question," or "Tell me in new words or different words." Then, I will ask the question with words you do understand.*

And if you do understand a question, you should answer it as best you can without guessing or making anything up, okay?

The following steps provide a guideline for practice:

1. Begin by clearly and concisely asking the child a question she does understand and does know the answer to, such as "What is your last name?" Wait for the child to answer.

- In the rare instance that a child puts out her hand to stop you or tells you she does not understand the question, remind her that she should do that only for those questions she does not understand, and that it is important for her to answer the questions she does understand.

- Then ask her another question she does understand, such as "How old are you?" If she answers accurately, praise her for thinking carefully about whether or not she understood the question and for answering the question she understood.

2. Next, ask the child one question while coughing, such as "[*coughing*] color [*coughing*]—day?" If the child tells you she does not understand the question (or puts her hand out to stop you), praise her for thinking about whether or not she understood the question and telling you she did not understand. Then ask the question again, using words that she can understand, such as "What color shirt/dress/pants are you wearing today?"

3. Continue by asking several questions using intelligible speech (i.e., without coughing or mumbling); these questions should vary in difficulty. Intersperse difficult-to-comprehend with easy-to-comprehend questions. See Table 7.1 for sample questions that are easy and difficult to understand.

4. Praise the child for answering questions she does understand and for informing you when she does not understand a question. Also, explicitly remind the child not to guess or make anything up if she does not understand a question. Many children catch on and start asking for a rephrase within a few questions.

Reducing Acquiescence: Strategies for Resisting Suggestion[1]

Children sometimes possess a number of expectations about task demands and adult intentions that can promote acquiescence rather than resistance to misleading questions. They underestimate adults' ability to make mistakes; overestimate adults' knowledge of events, even when the adult in question was not present at the event; anticipate that adults already know the answers to their questions (e.g., from external

Table 7.1 Sample Questions That Are Easy or Difficult to Understand

Sample easy questions

- "What foods do you like to eat for dinner?"

- "What do you like to do with your friends?"

- "What do you like to do on your birthday?"

Sample difficult questions

- "In what types of activities or experiences, chosen either by you, your siblings, or your parents, do you most enjoy engaging or participating in during holidays or during other extended periods when you are not required to be at school?"

    - *Rephrase*: May be rephrased as "What do you like to do on vacation?" if the child identifies the difficult sentence as incomprehensible.

- "Which of the various program options, either cable or commercial, that are not forbidden by your parents, do you most prefer to view?"

    - *Rephrase*: May be rephrased as "What is your favorite TV program?" if the child identifies the difficult sentence as incomprehensible.

- "Which food item, regardless of the time of day or occasion on which it is typically consumed, do you most want to not eat?"

    - *Rephrase*: May be rephrased as "What food do you hate the most?" if the child identifies the difficult sentence as incomprehensible.

sources children are not privy to); and express concern about adults being displeased or thinking less of the child if the child admits lack of knowledge or memory (e.g., "She'll think I'm stupid"). Although interviewers do their best to phrase questions in as non-leading a fashion as possible, some children benefit from increased awareness of the fact that interviewers may inadvertently put their guess into a question; that interviewers want to be informed of their mistakes; and children are not expected to answer every question substantively but can admit lack of knowledge or memory without disappointing the interviewer.

This section offers sample language as well as a practice task that interviewers may use if they deem the child would benefit from more exposure to these concepts. Again, the sample language and activities that follow are a completely optional element of the DNE that should be used only in cases where the interviewer deems them to be necessary or potentially beneficial.

Rationale for Admitting Lack of Knowledge and Correcting the Interviewer

To clarify task demands and provide the child with a rationale, children are told that questions might be misleading because an adult may put her guess into the question or make a mistake. Children are told that since the adult was not present at the event in question, she could not know what really happened. Sample language follows:

> *Sometimes when grownups ask children questions, a grownup might put her guess about what happened into a question, or she may make a mistake.*

> *For example, if I asked you "What was the name of the dog you played with in the waiting room?" would I be making a mistake about what really happened in the waiting room?* [Wait for the child to answer.] *And if you made up an answer, I could get confused about what really happened.*

To highlight adult expectations, and to disabuse children of the notion that they are required to respond to every question with a concrete substantive answer, you may want to use the following language:

> *Some questions might be easy, but some might be difficult. I do not expect you to know the answer to every question or to remember everything. But if you know the answer, tell the answer.*

Teaching the Self-Talk Strategy

Children are encouraged to talk to themselves when confronted with challenging questions; children are encouraged to use the following self-statements:

(a)   "Let me stop and think, what is the answer?"

(b)   "I'll rewind the video in my head to help me remember."

(c)   "This is hard, but I knew there would be questions like this: I can do it."

Sample language follows.

- *If I make a mistake or say something wrong when I ask you questions, I want you to correct me. Tell me I made a mistake. If I say something wrong, tell me it's wrong.*

- *You can talk to yourself and say: "Let me stop and think about what is the answer"; then rewind the video in your head to think about what really happened.*

- *Take your time and don't hurry. If a question is hard and you need to think about it, you can tell yourself "I knew there would be some questions like this one. I can do it."*

- *Then tell me the answer if you know it. Say "I don't know" if you don't know the answer; say "I don't remember" if you don't remember what happened; or say "No, that's wrong" if I say something that is wrong.*

- *It is important for you to tell me if I make a mistake. I want you to correct me. Tell me I made a mistake. If I say something wrong, tell me it's wrong. It is also important for you to tell me if you just don't know the answer, or if you don't remember. But if you know the answer, tell the answer.*

Place the emphasis on the child telling the answer if he knows it. Be sure to end with this admonition.

Using Thinking Cards to Clarify Response Options

For many children, the preceding instructions will be all that is necessary. They just need to be aware of the fact that interviewers may put their guess into a question and be given permission to say "I don't know" or to correct the interviewer. However, if a child appears confused and distracted, or overwhelmed by verbal options, you can consider using a set of visual cues we refer to as Thinking Cards to make children's response options explicit. Each card is a simple drawing that represents an acceptable response. The drawings appear in Appendix E and can be photocopied and cut into individual cards. These thinking cards are *not* used in the actual interview. They are merely available to help a subset of children concretize and clarify the response options if you deem it necessary.

As you tell the child the four response options above, you can show the card that represents the response:

(a) "I don't know." [*Show the picture of someone shrugging their shoulders.*]

(b) "I don't remember." [*Show the picture of someone rubbing her forehead.*]

(c) "No that's wrong." [*Show the picture of someone holding out her hand like a police officer stopping traffic.*]

(d) "Tell the answer if you know the answer." [*Show the picture of someone smiling and showing the "OK" sign.*]

Appendix E displays the four Thinking Cards used to make children's response options explicit.

Optional Practice for the Strategy

Some children may benefit from practice in answering a few leading and non-leading questions, the answers to which the child could not possibly know or remember. Steps with sample language follow:

1. *Let's practice for a moment* [Lay the four cards out on the table in front of the child, in cases where you decide to use them]. *You can whisper to yourself to help you answer a few questions.*

2. Then, briefly provide the child with an opportunity to say "I don't know" (e.g., asking the child what the interviewer's favorite food is); "I don't remember" (e.g., asking the child what he had for dinner a month ago); "that's wrong" (e.g., asking a question that assumes misinformation); or to answer the question (e.g., asking the child to tell you the names of his family members).

3. As always, be sure to praise the child's effort, not specific content. Say something like, *That was excellent; You listened*

carefully and tried hard; and you also told me when you didn't know or remember something, and you told the answer when you knew the answer.

Conclusions and Cautions

This chapter offers sample language and tasks for two optional elements of the DNE that are designed to improve accuracy of children's memory reports by reducing miscommunication and acquiescence to misleading questions. It is important to state once more that the DNE is not designed to use all of the optional components in every interview. Too much time spent in the beginning before initiating the core interview might reduce some children's later productivity because their attention span and cognitive resources are limited. Interviewing children is a complex and challenging task. Interviewers will need to observe children during the preliminaries and rapport-building phase to judge whether to include any of the optional DNE components described in the previous chapter or in this one.

Phase II Using the Developmental Narrative Elaboration Interview to Elicit Children's Statements

Chapter 8 | *The Core Developmental Narrative Elaboration Interview*

Materials Needed

Reminder Cards (optional)

Outline

- Conduct Step 1: Provide opportunity for spontaneous statement by child

- Conduct Step 2: Cued elaboration on event categories

- Conduct Step 3: Follow-up questions to elicit further detail

- Continuously evaluate when to proceed and when to terminate

Introduction

Phase II of the DNE interview provides an overarching three-step process for questioning children that has a clearly defined goal but a flexible process; it is not a script or a rigid protocol. Instead, you operate within certain guidelines but you are free to choose—from a toolkit of techniques—which methods to deploy as the interview unfolds. These can be applied according to the specifics of the case and the statements and behavior of the child that emerge during the interview.

With the DNE, you can change course when new information arises, dismiss old hypotheses and formulate new ones, discontinue strategies, and test alternative explanations for allegations. You can return to information mentioned by children for further elaboration, clarification, and explanation. Although the exact questions will not be specified before-hand, a good deal of thought should be given in advance to the specific topics likely to be addressed in a given interview and the method you will use for documentation of the content and process of the interview. In this chapter we describe the three steps of the core DNE, where the focus is on the process of eliciting children's memories, perceptions, and explanations regardless of the content. In the next chapter we will demonstrate how to apply these processes to cases of suspected child physical abuse, sexual abuse, and neglect, specifically.

The Core Interview: A Three-Step Process

The core interview involves three steps (see Table 8.1).

Overall, the three-step process of the core interview follows the commonly recommended approach of beginning with opportunities for spontaneous statements and using the least-leading, most open-ended, general prompts before moving to more specific questions, seeking the most accurate information from a young child, even if not the most detailed.

However, it is Step 2 that makes the DNE different from other interview formats and elicits detailed and relevant elaboration. Other protocols typically ask children for free recall of events and then move directly into detailed, potentially leading questions that might distort children's

Table 8.1 Three Step Process of Core Interview

Step 1—Free Recall	Create an opportunity for free recall of forensically relevant event(s) followed by simple, open-ended prompts for elaboration (i.e., "What happened next?" or "Tell me more about that.").
Step 2—Cued Elaboration	Provide an additional opportunity for elaboration on the child's narrative in response to four visual or verbal retrieval cues regarding participants, setting, actions, and conversations and affective states.
Step 3—Follow-up Questions	Use short answer follow-up questions to promote further elaboration, explanation, and clarification, phrased in a developmentally sensitive, non-leading fashion to generate multi-word responses.

statements. The DNE inserts an extra step between free recall and specific follow-up questions, which gives the child a chance to elaborate on his initial narrative in his own words, and during which the interviewer helps the child structure his memory search. The interviewer provides either verbal or visual retrieval cues that are empirically demonstrated to help children retrieve additional accurate information that they typically fail to report on their own when retelling narratives. This step provides interviewers with a larger data set of information from which to craft better-informed, and potentially less-biased, follow-up questions in Step 3 than would otherwise be possible.

Step 3 also follows the general principle of reserving specific questions until open-ended requests for multi-word responses are exhausted. However, rather than viewing the follow-up questioning phase as a funnel from least to most specific questions, as some experts have recommended, we have found that more often follow-up questioning resembles a series of small funnels as various topics or events are raised and explored, dropped, and reintroduced. In Step 3, as described below, interviewers double back to explore important points with requests for further elaboration, clarification, and justification. When questions that can be answered with one word are deemed necessary (e.g., *yes* or *no* or with another one-word answer), interviewers immediately follow children's answers with open-ended prompts that require children to further explain, justify, or clarify their one-word responses.

Step 1: Create Opportunities for Spontaneous Statements

Interviewer Note

From the beginning, provide children with the opportunity to make a spontaneous statement. Give them the impression that the interview is a joint effort and you want the child to do the talking.

Openings

Start by creating an opportunity for a relatively spontaneous statement in response to a non-leading, open-ended invitation; this should be a routine procedure. Not doing so undermines the child's credibility in the court case, which is a disservice to both the child and the process. Be sure to document the effort, even if the child does not respond with forensically relevant information. The first of such opportunities may have happened during rapport-development when the interviewer tells the child he would like to get to know the child better, and asks the child to talk about events/activities/people that are important to the child. For example, a spontaneous description of something of forensic relevance may occur in response to questions such as the following: "I would like to get to know you better. Tell me about something that is important to you." or "Now that you know my job is to help families solve problems and to keep children safe, is there anything you think I should know to do my job?" or "Now that you know the judge's job is to make the best plan for your family, is there anything I should tell the judge?"

Openings such as those listed in Table 8.2 provide additional opportunities.

Follow-up

If children respond with information that might be forensically relevant, encourage them to describe the event in their own words. Use open-ended questions such as "Tell me more" or "What happened?" that call for multi-word responses rather than forced-choice questions or questions that call for a "yes" or "no" response. When children stop describing, you can wait a few seconds and then prompt them once more, with general questions such as:

- *What happened next?*

- *And then what happened?*

- *Tell me more about that.*

- Repeat something the child said with a rising intonation to imply you are asking the child to elaborate.

During the child's narrative, refrain from interrupting, even if there are inconsistencies, contradictions, or irrelevant comments in the child's

Table 8.2 Step 1: Create Open-ended Opportunities for Spontaneous Statements

Once you have explained your role, the child's role, and the interview purpose, the following questions may be sufficient for children to independently raise topics of forensic interest.

- "How can I help you?"
- "What would you like to talk about today?"
- "What is on your mind today?"
- "Why do you think you are here today?"
- "Is there something you want to tell me/ talk with me about today? What?"
- "What made someone bring you here today?"
- "Is there something important we should talk about today?"
- "Is there something I can help you with? What?"
- "Is there something you want me to tell the judge or the lawyers? Something you want them to know?"
- "Is there anything I should know to do my job better? What is it?"
- "Is there something you can tell me to help me do my job? What is it?"
- "Is there something you don't want to talk to me about? What's that about? Help me understand the reasons you don't want to talk about something today."

If a few of these questions are not successful, you can get the conversation started by asking the child to tell you about some of the things in his or her life that are important to him or her:

- "Tell me about something important to you."
- "Tell me about some of the things you do (activities) that are important to you."
- "Tell me about some of the people in your life who are important to you."

statements. Below we describe how to double back later for elaboration and clarification as necessary in Step 3.

Note-taking

Keeping notes during the interview will be useful for this purpose even if the interview is documented electronically. In any event, write down the child's initial statement in her own words (as close to verbatim as possible) to guide follow-up questions. If she looks concerned about your note-taking, remind her that what she is saying is important and you do not want to forget or misremember. Referring to your notes later will help you remember accurately.

Give children plenty of time to respond. Go out of your way to be sure that the child has said everything she intends to say, even waiting until she says "That's all" at the end of her initial narrative. However, there is a balance between patiently allowing a child time to think and implying that her responses are inadequate (which is to be avoided).

Step 2: Cued Elaboration on Event Categories

Interviewer Note

Once the child has raised a forensically relevant topic, help the child elaborate on his own words by asking him to expand on the four event categories (Participants, Setting, Actions, Conversations and Affective States).

The event categories may be presented to the child by the verbal cues or through presentation of the four visual-cue cards (Reminder Cards) as described below.[1]

Using Verbal Category Cues

Since researchers have phrased verbal cues differently in various studies, all of which have been shown to improve children's reports, the results are fairly robust despite differences in wording. Below we outline two options for verbal cueing when you choose to use verbal instead of visual cues and forgo the pre-interview practice.

Option 1: Simple Verbal Cues

You can simply ask the four questions below, beginning with "Now I have a few more questions for you that might help you to tell some more about what you remember."

i.   *Tell me more about all of the people who were there and how the people looked.*

2. *Tell me more about where it was and how the place looked.*

3. *Tell me more about what happened, and what all of the people did.*

4. *Tell me more about what all of the people said and how they felt.*

Option 2: Simple Verbal Cues Plus Prompting

Another option is to employ a little more prompting on each category, using a few open-ended prompts beginning with "Wh-" questions. Sample questions follow:

- **Participants**: *Tell me more about the people who were there and how they looked:*

  - *Who was there?*
  - *What were their names?*
  - *What did each person look like?*
  - *You said [name of person identified] was there, what did [name of person] look like?*

- **Location(s)**: *Tell me more about where it happened:*

  - *Where were you?*
  - *What was the place you were in?*
  - *What did the place look like?*

- **Actions**: *Tell me more about what the people did.* [Or] *Tell me more about what each person did.*

  - *Tell me more about what* [name of person child identified] *was doing.*
  - *What did* [name of person child identified] *do with his/her hands? . . . with his/her feet?*
  - *How did* [name of person child identified] *move?*

- **Conversations**: *What did the people say?* [Or] *What did* [name of person child identified] *say?*

  - *What words did* [name of person child identified] *say?*
  - *What did you say?*

- **Emotional states of participants**: *How did the people feel?* [Or] *How did* [name of persons child identified] *feel?*

  - *What made you think* [name of person child identified] *felt that way?*
  - *What was* [name of person child identified] *doing/saying to make you think so?*

Note that whenever you mention someone's name, you should refer back to the child's previous statement that indicated that the person was present at the event (e.g., "You said John was there; what did John say to you?"). You should not introduce potential participants not yet mentioned by the child at this phase. Table 8.3 provides samples of simple, open-ended "Wh-" questions for each category. There are also examples of "Wh-" inquiries about sensations, timing, objects, and contexts as discussed in subsequent sections.

Using Visual Category Cues with Reminder Cards

If a child has practiced using the Reminder Cards previously,

1. Pull out the stack of four cards, saying:

   These cards may help you remember more, but they may not.

2. Then present each card individually prompting as described in Option A or Option B:

Option A

- Present each card individually with the following single open-ended prompt:

  Does this card remind you to tell something else?

- After child responds, move on to the next card.

Option B

- Present each card individually with an expanded prompt along the following lines:

- **The People Card:** *Does this card remind you to tell something more about who was there and what the people looked like? Who was there? How did each person look?*

Table 8.3 Step 2: Cued Elaboration

Categories	Sample Questions
Participants	Who was there? What people were there? What are their names? You said Nora was there; what did Nora look like? What did Nora's hair look like? Was anyone else there? Who?
Locations	Where did it happen? Tell me about the place. What did it look like? Was it inside or outside? What is the name of the room? What did the room look like? What was in the room?
Actions	You said Joan was there; what did she do? You said Mark was there; what did he do with his hands? How did he move his hands? Was anyone else there? What did they do?
Conversations	What did the people say? You said Tanika was there; what did Tanika say? What did Tanika tell you? What words did Tanika use? What did Tanika say to you? What did you say to Tanika?
Affective States	You said Mark was scared. What did Mark do that made you think he was scared? How did Mark show he was scared? What did Mark say to make you think he was scared?
Sensations	What did you see/hear/feel? What did that feel like? How did that feel? You said you got hurt. How did you get hurt? Where did you hurt; which body part hurt? Did it look different after it got hurt? How was it different? Was there a mark on your skin? How did it look? What made it hurt? Tell me how it felt when you got hurt? You said Mark was touching you; what body part did Mark use? How did Mark move his hands? Sometimes things go fast or slow, or they feel soft or hard, or they feel rough or smooth. How did it feel in the beginning? How did it feel at the end?
Timing	You said Mary came in; what was happening when Mary came into the room? You said the TV was on when it happened. What show was on TV when it happened? Tell me about the day it happened. Tell me what you did that day from the time you got up until the time you went to bed. Did this happen one time or more than one time? Did the same thing or almost the same thing happen another time? Tell me about that time.
Objects	What did Mark have in his hand? What did it look like? How did Mark use it? What did Mark do with it? How did it work? What made Mark pick it up? What made Mark put it down?"
Context	How did it begin/start? How did it end? How did it turn out? What happened right before? What happened right after? What did you do when it was over? What did Mark do when it was over? What happened when it was over?

- **Place Card:** *Does this card remind you to tell something more about where it happened and what it looked like? Where were you? How did the place look?*

- **What People Did Card:** *Does this card remind you to tell more about what each person did? What did each person do? What did the people do?*

- **Talking Feeling Card:** *Does this card remind you to tell more about what the people said and how they felt? What did the people say? How did the people feel? What were the people thinking?* [Then follow up with] *What makes you think so? What did the person say/do to make you think that?*

Note: If, when you are presenting any of the individual reminder cards, a child responds "No," implying the card does not remind him to tell anything else, then you should simply move on to the next card.

Also, sometimes young children respond by saying they cannot remember everything. If this happens, prompt with "Just tell me what you do remember."

A few pointers to keep in mind regarding the use of cards:

- You should not use the cards unless you have introduced them and practiced using them once at the end of the preliminary phase, before the core interview begins. Otherwise, they may be confusing to some children. So if you do decide not to do the pre-interview practice, use the verbal cues as described above.

- If the child has denied any forensically relevant event has taken place, do not use the cards to pressure the child to guess what might have happened or to confabulate.

- While the cards do not need to be used in a particular order, we have used the following order most often in our studies: *Participants, Setting, Actions,* and *Conversations/Affective State.* The advantage of starting with the participant category is that you can refer to the proper names of the participants later when asking about their actions, conversations, and affect states.

Step 3: Follow-up Questions to Elicit Further Detail

Interviewer Note
Return to important, vague, or inconsistent information raised by the child for further elaboration, clarification, and explanation in the child's own words using simple, short-answer questions.

Formulate follow-up questions according to guidelines that avoid suggestive methods, phrase questions in language children comprehend, and match the cognitive demands of the question to the child's level of development.

Returning to Important Information to Elicit Elaborative Details Using Short, Simple *Who*, *What*, *When*, *Where*, *How* Questions

To elicit further details, first try open-ended short-answer questions that require a multi-word response and preface each question by referring to information previously reported by the child (e.g., "You said ___ happened. Tell me more about that"). Use questions that start with "What," "Where," "When," "How," or "How Come/Why"—questions that force children to elaborate in their own words, rather than verify interviewer assumptions embedded into specific questions. For example:

■ *You said Jim was there. What did Jim do? What did that look like? What did you see/hear? How did that happen? What did Jim say? What words did he use? What happened in the beginning?...the end? What did Jim do with his hands?*

■ *You said Jim had a bat. What did Jim do with the bat? How did he move it? What made that happen? Who else was there? Who knows about what happened? How did it start? What made it stop?*

■ *You said there was a knife—what happened with the knife? Where did it come from? Who was holding it? What did* [the person holding it] *do with the knife? How did* [the person holding it] *move it? When did* [the person holding it] *pick it up?...put it down? What did that look like? How do you know he had a knife? Anyone else see it? Who? What did that person do/say?*

Requests for Firsthand Observations

Encourage the child to elaborate on firsthand observations and bodily sensations by repeating the child's comment, followed by prompts, such as the following:

■ *What did it look like? What did you see?*

■ *What did you hear?*

- *How did that feel? What made you feel that way?*

- *How did that happen? What made that happen?*

- *What were you thinking when that happened? What made you think that way?*

Again use simple, short, "Wh-" questions.

Exploring the Context (Antecedents and Consequences) of an Event

To fully understand the context of an incident, you will want to know what happened before and after the event and how it concluded. Since young children have difficulty with the linguistic use of *before* and *after*, you can ask how it started, and how it ended or stopped, or how it turned out. For example:

INTERVIEWER: You said ___ happened: how did it start?

CHILD: We were in the bathroom and he was helping me clean up the bathroom after my bath.

INTERVIEWER: How did it end?

CHILD: He cleaned up the rug.

INTERVIEWER: Why did he do that?

CHILD: Because I threw up after he made me suck him.

Requests for Explanation

Elaboration is often aided by prompts that request explanation and justification, such as "What makes you think so?" or "How did you learn that?" to allow children to explain their reasoning in their own words and provide an opportunity to elicit information relevant to alternative explanations. (For younger children, "How did you learn that?" is preferable to asking "How do you know?"). These prompts can elicit comments like "I saw it; I heard it; I felt it. He told me," which provide firsthand, personal detail. Again use simple, short "Wh-" questions.

Asking Children to Draw a Picture with Their Words

To avoid misunderstandings, repeat the child's comment followed by "What did it look like when that happened?" This request asks children to make a picture with their words so you can visualize what happened. In turn, this helps you paint a more specific picture of what you are asking with your follow-up questions. For example, when you say, "You said he touched you. Which part of your body did he touch?" you are directing the child's attention and memory search to simple, observable information that requires him to draw no inferences. This kind of elaboration often serves to clarify inconsistency or misinterpretation.

Exploring Repeated Events

In our studies we have only examined reports of single events. In some cases, however, there may be allegations of many repetitions, such as repeated sexual abuse over years. Once questioning about the initial event is finished, you may want to circle back to ask children to elaborate the other times similar events occurred. You can consider asking the child whether the event happened "one time or more than one time," "again," or "another time." You may want to ask whether the same thing or almost the same thing happened another time. Readers are encouraged to stay abreast of ongoing research regarding the best ways to help children identify, label, and elaborate repeated incidents, as well as to discriminate among repeated instances (e.g., how one incident was the same or not the same (different) from the others).

In our experience, children sometimes describe the generic script, that is, how it usually happened. When this happens, our advice is to allow children to provide this generic narrative before asking for elaboration on individual incidents. Once a second incident is identified or labeled, interviewers may want to go back and start the process again, using the four event category-cues to aid further elaboration on the second incident (Step 2) followed by short answer Wh- questions that require multiword responses (Step 3) (e.g.,

"You told me it happened the same way one more time/another time. Who was there? Tell me about who was there? Where did it happen? Tell me more about where it happened. You mentioned it happened again in the bathroom. Tell me more about how it happened in the bathroom. You said Jim was there. What did Jim do/say/feel? What did Jim do with his hands? You said he told you to do something, what words did he use? You said he was mad; what made you think he was mad? What did you do/say/feel?" and so forth). Also, you may want to ask children how this time was different from or the same as the first time they mentioned.

Exploring Timing of an Event

When exploring timing of events, remember that for young children (certainly those under eight to nine years of age) you should avoid asking for exact times of day unless you first establish the child's ability to tell time. Typically, children learn to tell time as part of the first- or second-grade curriculum. You often need to infer the time of day, calendar date, or year from time-tagged material (e.g., Child: "That happened when we were living in the apartment because we already got rid of the white house but the new house wasn't ready yet"). Children as young as four years can locate events in terms of the time of day (e.g., "It happened in the morning on the way to school"), but ordering events over longer time periods is a skill that develops gradually, beginning closer to six to seven years of age. Providing narratives in chronological order is a skill mastered closer to 10 years of age.

As mentioned previously, children may have difficulty with the way the terms *before* and *after* are used grammatically. Saywitz et al. (1992) found that asking children what happened *right* before or *right* after avoids one of these problems. Still, many elementary school–aged children have difficulty reporting whether an event occurred before or after a major holiday. Time-sensitive information may be reported in response to questions about the child's grade in school or the name of a teacher; which home was lived in during the target time period; weather, clothing, or accoutrements related to weather or season; and the age of the child or sibling. Younger children might be able to relate the day of the week to a special event, and you can ask them to explain why they think something occurred on a particular day. For example:

CHILD: It was Sunday.

INTERVIEWER: What makes you think so?

CHILD: We went to church in the morning.

In one case, an interviewer inferred the time of day because the child said while he was being abused he could hear the theme song of a particular television show playing in a different room. The investigator used *TV Guide* to obtain the half-hour window of opportunity.

Clarifying Children's Inconsistencies

To clarify inconsistencies, ask for the child's help. You can say something like the following:

- *You said ___, but I don't understand what you mean. I don't get it. Tell me in new words . . . tell me in a new way.*

- *I'm confused. Help me understand. A little bit ago you said ___. Now I heard you say ___. Can you help me understand what you mean?*

Remember that young children can have difficulty holding two comments in mind at once to compare or contrast. Often, young children benefit from non-leading prompts that provide them an opportunity to elaborate on individual pieces of previously mentioned information.

Again, asking children to explain their reasoning or how they gained their knowledge with a prompt such as "What makes you think so?" or "How did you learn that?" can be helpful in eliciting information relevant to alternate explanations for reports.

Clarifying Children's Evaluative and Idiosyncratic Comments

When children make evaluative comments (e.g., "That was bad"; "He's a bad man") or unbelievable idiosyncratic statements (e.g., "Glue came out of his penis"), or when they offer their own conclusions (e.g., "That would never happen"), elicit more objective information by asking them to clarify what they actually observed and to explain their reasoning process. For example:

- *You said he was bad: what did he **do** to **show** he was bad?*

- *You said that would never happen: why not? What makes you think that way?*

- *How do you know? How did you learn that?*

In one case, an eight-year-old girl spontaneously commented that the suspect was "mad." When asked, "What makes you think Joe was mad?" she responded, "Because he yelled at my sister when she opened the door while he was doing it to me and told her to get out." She thus revealed the presence of another witness to the alleged crime.

Clarifying the Source of Children's Knowledge

To understand fully children's comments, you often have to ask them about the sources of their knowledge. This is not the kind of information young children report spontaneously. When children say they were told something, ask what words were used. When children say they know something, ask if they saw or heard someone do or say it. These sources include the following:

- **How they gained the knowledge they have**: *How do you know that? How did you learn that? Did you see it? What did you see? Did someone tell you about it? What did he say? What makes you think that?*

- **Who else has the knowledge**: *Who else knows about what happened? Did anyone else see it happen?*

- **How the other person obtained the knowledge**: *How did he find out? How did he learn about it?*

- **How the child knows the other person has the knowledge**: Interviewer: *What makes you think he knows?* Child: *I told him.* Interviewer: *What words did you use?*

- **Who else the child told, thinks he told, or tried to tell about what happened**: *Did you tell anyone about what happened? Who? What words did you use?*

- **How that person reacted**: *What did your aunt do/say when you told her? How did she feel? What makes you think so?*

Clarifying Vague Comments

When children's comments are vague, clarification efforts can focus their attention on their own observations and firsthand experience and sensations. Explore descriptions of movements (*What made it start? What made it stop? How did he move? What body parts did he use?*) and the physical characteristics of actions (fast, slow, hard, soft). For example, one interviewer's questions captured a child's difficulty breathing as an adult put pressure on her chest during sexual intercourse

CHILD: I couldn't breathe.

INTERVIEWER: What stopped you?

CHILD: He kept pushing up and down on me.

INTERVIEWER: How did he do that?

CHILD: Really fast like he was jumping on me with his whole body.

INTERVIEWER: What did that feel like?

CHILD: It hurt my chest.

When children try to explain other people's behaviors, young children's explanations can be fragmentary and vague, creating more confusion than clarity. Their ability to infer other's motivations and intents can be limited by their immaturity in drawing causal inferences from outward behaviors and circumstances. Younger children often use global terms that require further inquiry to understand what the other person said or did to make the child think he was, for example, "nice" or "mean." Ask the child to describe the behaviors or statements he *saw* and *heard* to make him think a person was nice or mean. Ask what the person did to *show* he felt a certain way. For example, one five-year-old who initially said "I don't know" when asked how she obtained her bruises also described her 15-year-old sibling as mean, but elaborated further when asked "What did he do to be mean? What were the mean things he did?" saying "He hits me and yells at me when my mom is out," providing an alternative explanation for her bruises to parental abuse.

Using Questions That Require One-Word Answers

Sometimes questions answerable with one word are deemed necessary. If so, follow the single-word response with a more general prompt that asks the child to elaborate further in his own words. For example:

INTERVIEWER: "Who takes care of you when your mom is gone/away?"

CHILD: "Mary."

INTERVIEWER: "Anybody else?"

CHILD: "Sometimes her boyfriend comes over, too."

INTERVIEWER: "Was he wearing all his clothes the whole time?"

CHILD: "No."

INTERVIEWER: "Did he take off some clothes?"

CHILD: "Yes."

INTERVIEWER: "What part of his clothing?"

CHILD: "His pants."

INTERVIEWER: "Does your grandma know what happened?"

CHILD: "No."

INTERVIEWER: "Was she home when it happened?"

CHILD: "Yes."

INTERVIEWER: "Did she see what happened?"

CHILD: "No."

INTERVIEWER: "Why couldn't she see what happened?"

CHILD: "She was asleep in her room."

Using *Yes/No* Questions

First, try to avoid yes-or-no questions ("Did he hit you?") by rephrasing them into open-ended "Wh-" questions ("What did he do with his hands?") that require children to describe observable behaviors and statements. When you do use a specific yes/no question, follow up immediately by returning to open-ended "Wh-" questions that require children to elaborate or explain their answer further. For example, when a child says yes to the question, "Was he holding something in his hands?" follow up with "Wh-" questions (e.g., Interviewer: "What was he holding?" Child: "A hammer." Interviewer: "What did he do with it?" Child: "Break the car window." Interviewer: "What happened next?"). Clarity will be enhanced by a series of short, simple "Wh-" questions rather than one overloaded question, the answer to which will be difficult to decipher. If a child says yes to the question "Did he touch you?" you can follow up with questions such as:

- *What happened? How did it happen? How did he touch you?*

- *What body part did he use? What did he do with his hands?*

- *What part of your body got touched? Where did he touch you?*

- *How did he touch you? How did he move?*

- *What did it look like?. . . feel like?. . . sound like?*

Using *Why* Questions

Children five to seven years of age and younger have a limited understanding of causality, so use "why" questions cautiously with children in this age group. When children provide questionable answers, consider rephrasing "why" questions as, for example, *How come?* or *What made that happen?* Or you can ask children to explain their reasoning with *What makes you think so?*

In addition, "why" questions often sound like attributions of blame, particularly when relating to the child's own behavior (e.g., "Why did you go to his house if you were afraid? Why didn't you try to run when you saw him closing the shades and locking the door?"); adults often ask children to explain the negative but not the positive ("Why did you get a D?" but never "Why did you get an A?"). Rephrase "why" questions to minimize implied accusation. For example, in an allegation of acquaintance rape, you could rephrase "Why did you go with him if you thought something bad might happen?" to "What thoughts did you have right before/after you went with him?"; "You said you were thinking you were afraid of him; what did he do that frightened you? When did you become afraid of him? What made you afraid of him? What did you do when you were afraid of him?" Table 8.4 provides sample follow-up questions in developmentally sensitive language for Step 3 of the core DNE.

Table 8.4 Step 3: Sample Follow-up Questions to Elicit Further Detail

---

Doubling Back for Clarification

When narration is complete, return to important, vague, or contradictory points for more information:

To clarify inconsistencies:

"I'm confused; help me understand better. I don't get it."

"Tell me in new words. Tell me another way."

To clarify evaluative comments:

"You said John was bad/good or mean/nice; what makes you think so?"

"What did John do to make you think that way?"

"How do you know?"

"What did John do to show you he was mean/nice?"

"What did John look like when he was being mean/nice?"

"What did John do/say when he was being mean/nice?"

To clarify child's source of knowledge:

"How do you know that?" "How did you learn that?"

"Did you see it?" "What did you see/hear?"

"Did someone tell you about it?" "What did he/she say?"

"Who else knows?"

"Did anyone else see it happen?" "Who else saw it happen?"

"How did your mom find out?" "How did she learn about it?"

"What makes you think your mom knows?"

"Did you tell anyone about what happened? Who?" "What did you say?"

"What did your aunt do/say when you told her?"

Suggestive Techniques to Avoid

In laboratory studies, certain types of questions and techniques tend to be responsible for most of the false information elicited from young children. These methods can usually be avoided with little loss of valuable information. The use of one or more suggestive questions in a single interview is unlikely to seriously distort a child's report, especially if you are unbiased and explore multiple hypotheses over the course of the interview (e.g., the whereabouts of other adults with access to the child during the same time frame, not only the suspect). However, if you expose a child to multiple suggestive techniques in repeated interviews and you pursue a biased hypothesis single-mindedly, children's reports can be seriously distorted. If a suspect is innocent, suggestive techniques applied this way can reinforce or promote false allegations. Even if there is physical evidence to suggest a perpetrator is guilty, such techniques will be rightfully challenged by the defense to discredit the child witness and the interviewer.

Tag Questions

Avoid tag questions that ask children to verify the interviewer's perspective; these tag questions are usually formed by adding a presumptive phrase to the end of a statement like "isn't that true?"; "wasn't it?"; or "didn't he/she/it?" (e.g., "He hit you, didn't he?" "It was Mr. Blick that fired the gun, wasn't it?" "You opened the door on your own, isn't that true?"). Tag questions disproportionately impair reports of children five years of age and younger.

Multiple-Choice Questions

Avoid multiple-choice questions that limit children's answers to choices suggested by you (e.g., "Did he use a knife, a hammer, a plunger, or some other thing?" "Was his shirt blue, green, red, or some other color?"). The more choices and the more complicated the task you give, the more likely you will exceed a young child's ability to remember all these choices.

Negation

Avoid questions that insert negatives into the body of the question (e.g., "Didn't he hurt you?") or tag it onto the end (e.g., "Your mom told you to stay away from there. Is that not true? Didn't she?"). Negative-term insertions increase error rates for both children and adults.

Suppositional Questions

Avoid forced-choice suppositional questions. They make presumptions without giving children an opportunity to affirm or deny the presumption and then force them to choose between two or more answers. These questions usually begin with a clause that assumes certain information as a given and then asks about a separate aspect of the event (e.g., "When he hit you, did he use a belt or his hand?"). When the given or implied information is misleading, children who try to answer the question are boxed into a corner. So, avoid multi-clause questions in which the first clause implies information of dubious reliability. Several short questions are less confusing and offer less room for suggestion than a single overloaded one.

Encouraging Children to Form a Negative Stereotype About Someone

Avoid making comments that suggest the suspect might be a "bad man" who did "bad things" (e.g., "I heard he was a mean bus driver"). Many studies highlight the importance of objectivity and an open mind in framing questions.

Peer Pressure

Avoid telling young children that their friends or classmates have already informed you about what happened. This can increase children's errors when used in combination with other suggestive techniques.

Parental Pressure

Avoid suggesting to a young child that parents have already told you what happened (e.g., "It's okay to talk to me, your mom already told me what happened") or suggesting what happened based on the word of a parent (e.g., "Your mom already told me that your dad does things you don't like when you visit him overnight. Tell me about what happens"). Since you are unaware of parent's motivations and biases, avoid mentioning their expectations or opinions when you question their children.

Table 8.5 Suggestive Techniques to Avoid

- Repeated suggestions that hold preconceived negative stereotypes of the accused (Interviewer: "He's a bad man. He did bad things.").

- Pursuing a single hypothesis single-mindedly based on preconceived bias.

- Putting peer pressure on children by telling them that other children have talked to you about similar activities.

- Rejecting a child's answer and insisting on a different one.

- Repeatedly asking children to visualize, imagine, or pretend what might have happened despite their denials (Interviewer: "I know you say it didn't happen to you, but pretend it did. Tell me how it might have gone. Think real hard.").

- Anatomical dolls and toys used with 3 and 4 year olds paired with suggestive questions and requests to re-enact events.

- Offering tangible rewards for specific answers.

Preconceptions

Studies of human reasoning suggest we tend to possess a *confirmatory bias*. That is, we overvalue and pay more attention to information that confirms our biases and preconceptions than to information that disconfirms them (Goodman & Melinder, 2007). Researchers have staged events with children and then led the interviewers to form inaccurate hypotheses about what probably happened (Goodman, Sharma, Thomas, & Considine, 1995; White et al., 1997). When unfamiliar interviewers are misinformed, they are at greater risk of asking more biased questions that can jeopardize the accuracy of children's responses. Table 8.5 describes additional suggestive techniques to avoid.

Phrasing Questions in Language Children Can Comprehend

As mentioned previously, Phase I is an opportunity to listen to a child's speech, grammar, and vocabulary for clues to match your language to a child's level of comprehension. Typically, if a child uses a language form correctly in his own speech, he will understand that form when others use it. So, during the initial conversation, listen for the number of words in a sentence, the number of syllables in a word, the complexity of the grammar, the sophistication of the vocabulary, and whether the child uses pronouns and tenses correctly. Then simplify your grammar and vocabulary according to the guidelines that follow.

Simplifying Your Grammar

✓ **Use shorter sentences**. Avoid long compound sentences. Rather than asking one overloaded question filled with details, try several simple, short questions to elicit the same information. Typically, overloaded questions are several questions disguised as one and assume a great deal of information yet to be verified by the child. Hence, the meaning of a child's single answer is often unclear.

✓ **Use simple sentence constructions**. Avoid embedded and relative clauses. Young children's comprehension does not run that far ahead of their production. It is not until closer to 10 years of age that children master many of the more difficult grammar rules.

✓ **Use one basic idea per utterance with young children.** Their sentences are rarely packed with multiple adjectives and adverbs (e.g., "The hot red sun set slowly"). Instead, extra information is conveyed through additional sentences (e.g., "The sun went down. It was hot. It was red. It was slow"). Similarly, communication is clearest when you use multiple simple questions (e.g., "What color was it?" "How did it move?").

✓ **Use simple tenses. Avoid multi-word verbs**. Children can only process so many words in an utterance, so use simple tenses (e.g., "was") rather than multi-worded verbs (e.g., "might have been"). You do not want to waste several words on verbs or clauses that won't be understood or remembered.

✓ **Use the active voice and not the passive voice.** Using the active voice will be more readily understood by children (e.g., say "You said he touched you. What part of your body did he touch?" rather than "Which part of your body was touched (by him)?").

✓ **Orient child when switching topics.** When moving to a new topic, announce that you are doing so (e.g., "Now I want to ask you about..."). Switching frames of reference without pointing it out to young children explicitly can result in confusion.

Simplifying Your Vocabulary

✓ **Use concrete, easily visualized terms rather than abstract terms.** For example, avoid terms that name the abstract category (e.g., *weapon*). Ask "What was Jon doing with his hands?" not "Was Jon holding a weapon?" Abstract terms may seem less biasing for adult witnesses but can be confusing for young children.

✓ **Use words with fewer syllables per word for younger children.** With children under age seven, one- to two-syllable words are preferable to three- to four-syllable words. Use a couple of one-syllable words (e.g., "point to") rather than one four-syllable word (e.g., "identify"). This will lessen the sophistication of your vocabulary naturally.

✓ **Use common terms and meanings.** Use terms the child is most likely to have heard, rather than infrequently used synonyms. Also use the meaning of the term that is most likely to be familiar to the child (e.g., to a young child, a "court" is a place to play basketball rather than a court of law). Avoid legal jargon.

✓ **Use proper names and avoid pronouns with young children.** With younger children, it is preferable to always use proper names (e.g., "Mary," "Jack") rather than pronouns ("him," "her," "he," "she"), no matter how tedious it seems to the adult. Prepositions and pronouns may not be fully mastered until children are seven years of age.

✓ **Clarify uncommon or complex terms in advance**. Be certain that children have the same meaning in mind as you do when using a term. Young children often use words in an idiosyncratic manner, especially words naming people, places, body parts, and time.

- Do not ask a young child if he knows what a certain word means. The child is likely to say yes, but may have a very different meaning in mind than you do (e.g., when asked, "Do you know what *allegation* means?" a child may answer "Yes" but be thinking about alligators).

- Ask older children (over seven years of age) to tell you what the word means in their own words. But do not ask younger children to provide definitions, especially of abstract concepts (e.g., "What does the word *allegation* mean?").

- When words are abstract, you can ask about exemplars. For instance, rather than asking what month an event occurred, be certain the child understands the concept of *month*. You can ask the child to verify statements as "true," "not true," or "don't know." For example, "June and July are names of months. True or not true?" "Susan and Jane are names of months. True or not true?"

Matching Questions to Children's Knowledge Base, Reasoning Abilities, and Academic Skills

In the forensic context there is often a mismatch between the kind of information a child can provide and the kind of precise answers the legal and social-service systems seek in order to make decisions about child protection and adult culpability. For example, when the system seeks to identify an unknown perpetrator or evaluate a suspect's alibi, and a child hasn't learned to use conventional units of measurement to answer "What time was it?" "How tall was he?" or "How much did he weigh?" there is fertile ground for misinterpretation of the child's attempt to answer. The guidelines that follow provide suggestions for matching the cognitive demands of your questions to a young child's knowledge base, academic skills, and reasoning abilities.

✓ **Use stable terms and avoid referents that change their meaning depending on time or place,** such as *here/there* and *yesterday/tomorrow*. For example, when someone is standing in the front of the room, he is "here," but if he walks to the back of the room, then the front of the room becomes "there." What was once "near" is now "far." What was to the child's "right" in one position is now to his "left" in another.

✓ **Be careful about asking if–then questions that require hypothetical-deductive reasoning**. Avoid asking young children questions that ask them to draw inferences beyond the information given.

✓ **Avoid relational and relative terms that require young children to make judgments in relation to a standard, a dimension, or a situation that can change** (e.g., *thick/thin, more/less*).

✓ **Be careful asking children to estimate distance, timing, weight, age, calendar dates, using conventional systems of measurement,** which children usually learn between the first and third grades. Be careful asking questions that require answers in terms of pounds, miles, feet, inches, calendar dates, months, minutes, and hours, and so forth.

✓ **Be careful asking young children to estimate something when it might involve using multiplication or division.** Multiplication or division are often not mastered until fourth and fifth grade, so be careful in asking how many times something happened (e.g., for example, if it happened every time Mom went to night-school class, which was two times a week for ten weeks, an estimate requires multiplication or complex addition).

✓ **Be careful asking children about precise locations requiring names of streets, cities, or states.** Again, geographical locations and maps are part of the elementary-school curriculum.

✓ **Be careful with some basic concepts not mastered fully until kindergarten or first grade,** including the following:

- first, last, never, always
- beside, before, after, top, over, next to, through
- front, away from, behind, row, between, bottom, widest, corner, side
- not many, most, every, whole, few, several
- above, below, beginning, alike

✓ **To avoid misinterpretation, remember that major kinship terms may not be understood fully until the child is age 10.** First, children master the terms for *mother, father, sister, brother*. However, although a four- year-old may know he *has* a brother, he may not know that he *is* a brother to his brother. Next children master the terms for *son, daughter, grandfather, grandmother,* and *parent.* Finally, they master *uncle, aunt, cousin, nephew,* and *niece* (Owens, 2011).

✓ **To avoid misinterpretation, remember that, before they fully understand a concept, children may use a term too restrictively or too broadly.** For example, a child may have narrow understanding of the term *touch* and may fail to report related actions, such as rubbing or pinching, when questioned about being touched; or a child may over-generalize from their limited experience, referring to all female caregivers as "mommies." When a child's answer does not make sense, consider this issue.

Continuously Evaluate When to Proceed and When to Terminate

At some point in the process of elaborating on an initial description, children may indicate they either do not remember any more (Interviewer: "Anything else?" Child: "No"); do not want to talk about it any further ("I'm done talking. That's enough." "Can I go now?"); or that there is something else they want to do or talk about (e.g., "Did you know I am the center on my basketball team? My game starts really soon. I gotta go."). When a child indicates his memory has been exhausted, be respectful. When children hesitate, show you are trying to understand their difficulty. Do not pressure children to continue. Instead, try to clarify the reason for their silence, avoidance, diversion, or refusal. For example:

INTERVIEWER: What's making it hard to talk?

CHILD: I don't remember any more about it. It was a long time ago.

INTERVIEWER: Sounds like it is hard to remember any more right now.

Cost–Benefit Analysis

There is a limit to the amount of detail a young child can be expected to provide on the spot. At various points in the interview, you should conduct a cost–benefit analysis of continuing further or scheduling a

Form 8.1 Checklist for Phrasing Questions in Language Children Can Comprehend

Simplify Your Grammar:
- ✓ Use shorter sentences.
- ✓ Use simple sentence constructions.
- ✓ Use one basic idea per utterance with young children.
- ✓ Use simple tenses. Avoid multi-word verbs.
- ✓ Use the active voice and not the passive voice.
- ✓ Orient child when switching topics.

Simplify Your Vocabulary:
- ✓ Use concrete, easily visualized terms rather than abstract terms.
- ✓ Use one- or two-syllable words rather than three- or four-syllable words for younger children.
- ✓ Use common terms and meanings. Avoid legal jargon.
- ✓ Use proper names and avoid pronouns with young children.
- ✓ Clarify uncommon or complex terms in advance.

Match Questions to Children's Knowledge Base, Reasoning Abilities, and Academic Skills:
- ✓ Use stable terms and avoid referents that change their meaning depending on time or place.
- ✓ Be careful about asking if–then questions that require hypothetical-deductive reasoning.
- ✓ Avoid relational and relative terms that require young children to make judgments in relation to a standard, a dimension, or a situation that can change.
- ✓ Be careful asking children to estimate distance, timing, weight, age, calendar dates, using conventional systems of measurement.
- ✓ Be careful asking young children to estimate when it might involve using multiplication or division, which may not be learned until fourth or fifth grade.
- ✓ Be careful asking children about precise locations requiring names of streets, cities, or states.
- ✓ Be careful with some basic concepts that are not mastered fully until kindergarten or first grade, including the following: first, last, never, always, beside, before, after, top, over, next to, through, front, away from, behind, row, between, bottom, widest, corner, side, many, most, every, whole, few, several, above, below, beginning, alike.
- ✓ To avoid misinterpretation, remember that major kinship terms may not be understood fully until children are age 10.
- ✓ To avoid misinterpretation, remember that before they fully understand a concept, children may use a term too restrictively or too broadly.

subsequent interview. Factors you should consider in determining whether to terminate include:

- the extent of physical or medical evidence or lack thereof
- the likelihood the child is in imminent danger and needs protection
- any motive for the child to fabricate or for adults to coach
- any motive for the child to recant or deny
- the number and quality of previous interviews

Avoid Pressuring

When children with no relevant experiences or memory are pressured, confabulation and false allegations can occur. When children indicate that nothing untoward has happened, you should respect their denials (e.g., Interviewer: "What happened when Mr. Z came over to your house?" Child: "Nothing. We watched TV. I told you. That's all"). Instead, you may want to back up ("What were you watching on TV?" or "What happened right before you started watching TV?"), or come at the topic in a more roundabout way ("Why did your social worker bring you here today instead of your mom?").

When genuine victims are pressured, recantations may be more likely. Pressuring young children can give the impression it is acceptable to invent information just to confirm your presumptions (e.g., Child: "I told you I don't know. Do you want me to guess or what?"). If you choose not to terminate the interview, it is best to back off and further deepen the rapport and your understanding of what the child finds important and the obstacles he faces. When emotional and motivational factors are at play (e.g., fear of retaliation, fear of rejection, or embarrassment), consider scheduling a follow-up interview. You can give children a way to contact you in case they think of something else they want to tell you later.

Introducing the Topic of Interest

When the procedures thus far have failed to raise the topic of interest, allegation, or suspicion, interviewers will need to weigh the merits and drawbacks of introducing information from other sources in a non-leading fashion. You can ask the child to explain why she came to see you and why other people might think it is a good idea for her to meet with you. You can consider introducing verifiable information from other sources, such as medical evidence (treatment for injuries), known locations and contexts of interest (e.g., preschool, church, relatives, babysitters), instances of previous disclosure, people to whom she has previously disclosed information, their reactions, or known contact with social service or law-enforcement professionals.

Conclusion

This chapter outlines the three-step process of conducting the core DNE interview. Step 1 is the opportunity for the child to give a relatively spontaneous description of something of forensic relevance.[2] It is an opportunity for free recall with minimal prompting from the interviewer. Step 2 is the step that makes the DNE interview unique. This is the step of cued elaboration. Interviewers insert, between free recall and specific follow-up questions, an extra opportunity for children to elaborate on their initial narrative in response to four category cues. Elaboration focuses on participants, setting, actions, conversations, and affective states, as well as elaboration of context, timing, objects, and sensory input. Step 3 is an opportunity to return to important information for further elaboration, clarification, or explanation with questions that require primarily multi-word responses. This chapter provides suggestions for phrasing questions in developmentally sensitive language and concepts; avoiding suggestive question types and techniques; and doubling back to clarify inconsistencies, vague or evaluative comments, antecedents, consequences, firsthand observations, and the source of the child's knowledge. In summary, this chapter focuses on the interview process regardless of the content of the case. The next chapter discusses how to apply this process in cases of suspected child abuse and neglect.

Chapter 9   *Exploring the Details in Allegations of Abuse and Neglect*

Materials Needed

None

Outline

- Explore patterns of maltreatment over time

- Explore previous statements, disclosures, and failure to disclose

- Explore alternative explanations for allegation

- Explore allegations of sexual assault

- Explore allegations of physical abuse

- Explore allegations of neglect, failure to protect, and lack of supervision

Introduction

In this chapter, we discuss areas for further exploration in cases of child maltreatment. We provide examples using the previously discussed DNE guidelines for constructing developmentally sensitive and non-suggestive follow-up questions that help children elaborate the details in their own words.

Exploring Patterns of Maltreatment over Time

If the basic interview reveals events of forensic relevance, you can estimate future risk by helping children elaborate on whether there is a pattern of abuse or neglect over time. To inquire about multiple incidents, ask:

- whether it happened one time or more than one time;

- whether the child was surprised it happened. If not surprised, ask how she knew it might happen (*What made you think it could happen? Were you worried it would happen?*);

- whether it happened to someone else the child knows (e.g., siblings) and how the child learned that it had happened; and

- whether other types of abuse (sexual, physical, and/or emotional) occurred before, during, or after the event in question.

Exploring Previous Statements, Disclosures, and Failure to Disclose

If evidence of maltreatment arises during the interview, it can be useful to help children elaborate on the following:

- Whether the child told or tried to tell anyone previously (*Did you tell anyone else? Who? What words did you use?*)

- Context in which that disclosure occurred (*What made you tell? Where... When...? What happened right before/after you told [person identified]?*)

- Person's reaction to being told (e.g., *What did Auny May say/do when you told her? Did Aunt May tell you to tell anyone else? Who? Why? Did Aunt May tell you to keep it a secret? Why do you think she did that?*)

- Outcome of the disclosure (*What happened after you told? What changed?*)

- If the child waited to tell:

    - Explore the reasons why the child decided to wait (Interviewer: *People usually have good reasons for what they do or don't do. You probably had a good reason for waiting to tell. What was it? Child: He said he would hurt my mom if I told anyone.*)

- Explore relevant fears; for example, fears of bodily harm, rejection, separation from caretaker, loss of love, removal from home, loss of privileges, or not being believed (*What were you worried about?* [or] *worried might happen if you told someone else? What made you worry about that?*)

- If there are past reports of maltreatment, explore whether and how the abuse stopped and started again, and how non-abusive caretakers reacted to any previous disclosure (e.g., *What made it stop?*)

Exploring Alternative Explanations for Allegation[s]

Sorting out alternative hypotheses often involves helping children elaborate on details that put the event in question into context. As mentioned previously, children may not spontaneously report the full context in which events occur because they fail to take the listener's limited knowledge base into account and fall short of fully orienting the listener to the appropriate context for interpreting the child's remarks. Hence, questions that explore the antecedents and consequences of forensically relevant events ("What happened right before and right after?"), as well as precipitating events ("What made her act that way? What made him angry or upset? What made him start doing that?... stop doing that?") can help children provide the contextual detail.

- To explore alternative suspects, elicit a list of people who have had access to the child (e.g., *What are the names of the grownups that take care of you? Baby-sit? After school? On the weekends?*).

- To distinguish abusive or neglectful behavior from caretaking of young children who need help toileting, bathing, and dressing, and who wander into dangerous situations on their own, try to place statements in the context of the child's overall life experience:

  - Ask about the kinds of problems the child has (problems with self-care activities, injuries, and other medical problems) and how the child solves them, such as getting help from grownups and siblings (*What would you do if you needed help? If you fell off your bike? If you got hurt? Who would you go to/tell? What do you think they would do? What kinds of problems have you had? What did you do? What happened?*).

- Explore who helps solve which problems, how they do it, and differences among the caretakers in terms of how they help the child with problems.

- Ask questions that differentiate whether the incident in question is a rare or frequent occurrence, unique to a particular adult or similar to experiences with other adults (*What do other grownups do when they help you? Did Bob do it the same way? How is it the same? How is it not the same?*).

- To assess the overall level of distress at home, ask what kinds of problems the family has faced and how other family members coped (e.g., deaths, substance-abuse by older sibling, parental separations, community violence).

- When neglect is suspected, explore evidence—such as erratic behavior, stumbling, unresponsiveness to children's overtures—that caretakers might be under the influence of drugs or alcohol, or be emotionally unstable (e.g., *Do you worry that your mom might hurt herself?. . . that she is not always safe? What might happen?*).

- When sexual abuse is suspected, ask about prior experience with nudity and sexual activity, including exposure to sexualized or aggressive television or videos, typical bathing and toileting procedures with alleged perpetrator and other caretakers, family attitudes regarding nudity and sexuality, and whether other caretakers engage in behaviors similar to the alleged perpetrator's.

Exploring Allegations of Sexual Assault

Below is a brief list of topics interviewers might want to use in formulating follow-up questions when a child is referred for suspicion of sexual assault. It is not a comprehensive list, and there is no set order in which to explore topics. Table 9.1 displays a sampling of developmentally sensitive questions that illustrate how to explore some of the items on this list.

Table 9.1 Sample Questions Regarding Allegations of Sexual Abuse

■ **Sexualized Acts:**

What did Tom do with his body/fingers/hands? You said there was kissing—what body parts got kissed? What did he do with his lips? Was there licking/sucking/rubbing/touching? Tell me more about it. How did his body move around? What body parts did Tom use/move? You said Tom rubbed you on your private parts—did Tom rub you on top of your clothes?...under your clothes? What were you thinking right before Tom started rubbing you on your private parts? What did Tom do to make you start to get worried? You said Tom used his wiener. What did Tom do with his wiener? How did Tom move it? How did it look?...feel? You said Tom put something on his wiener; what was it? What did it look like? Where did it come from? What happened to it at the end? Did anything else happen to/with Tom's wiener? What? Did it change from the beginning to the end?

■ **Sensory Input:**

You said Tom made noises—what kind of noises did Tom make? What was Tom doing when he made the noises? What did it sound like? Did the noises change over time? You said Tom was yelling, what did Tom yell about? What words did Tom use?

■ **Nudity and Undressing:**

You said you were scared—what were you wearing when you started to get scared? Did you wear all of your clothes the whole time/all the time? You said Tom took off his pants—did Tom tell you to take your clothing off, too? What words did Tom use? How come Tom did that? What piece of clothes stayed on?...came off? Did you see Tom's private parts? Were all your private parts under your clothes?

■ **Force:**

You said you told Tom to stop—what did Tom do when you told him to stop? What do you think is the reason Tom did not stop? What words did you use? What words did Tom use?

■ **Pornography:**

You said Tom put on a movie—what did you see on the movie? Where did it come from? Did people have their clothes on in the movie? What happened? Did people take their clothes off in the movie? What happened? Did you see their private parts? Tell me more. When did Tom stop the movie?

■ **Drugs and Alcohol:**

You said you felt dizzy—what made you feel dizzy? When did you first start feeling dizzy? Did you eat or drink anything? What? How did it taste?...smell? You said John was acting funny—what made you think so? What was he doing or saying that made you think he was acting funny? Did he fall down or stumble? Did you think he might hurt himself? Were you worried someone would get hurt? What made you worried? What did you see or hear that made you worry about someone getting hurt?

■ Description of sexual or aggressive actions (e.g., fondling, attempted penetration...):

■ Body parts and positions involved
■ Elicit the child's terms for body parts (what a part is called/named) and knowledge of body functions (what each part does).

Children use a wide range of slang terms for private parts.

- Types of movements (e.g., hard, soft, fast, hitting, rubbing, pushing, grabbing)
- Sensory input (e.g., pain, itching, wetness, bleeding, noises heard, tastes of drugs, alcohol, semen…)
- Use of force or coercion to gain compliance (threats, gifts, bribes…)
- Use of objects (e.g., sexual devices, contraceptives, lubricants, or pornography)

- Name and physical description of alleged offenders or other victims and witnesses

- Context of what happened:

  - Antecedents and Consequences (e.g., "How did it start? How did it end? Was it during bath time, bedtime…? What happened when it was over?")
  - Adult verbalizations or explanations given for removing clothes (e.g., "game" and how game was played) or engaging in sexualized activities (e.g., hygiene, education)
  - Where family members and caretakers were at the time of the incident
  - Child's reaction to the incident
  - Other types of abuse present (emotional, physical)
  - Exploration of past injuries, kinds of pain experienced, and what kind of medical treatment was sought to help place statements in context

- Explore evidence of:

  - enticements, promises, threats
  - drugs, alcohol
  - photography, pornography, cellphone video
  - interruptions, failed attempts
  - lubricants, contraceptives
  - ejaculation, bleeding
  - descriptions of cleaning up afterwards

- Explore exposure to live sexual activity, or allegations of witnessing other victims being abused.

- Explore evidence of age-inconsistent sexual knowledge and behavior:

  - Although not proof of abuse, there are significant legal implications when very young children demonstrate detailed knowledge of sexual activities that most children their age do not possess (e.g., increased pace of breathing leading to orgasm).
  - Although it is not uncommon for children to exhibit sexualized behavior, such as masturbation and exploratory games with peers in ongoing relationships that are voluntary and devoid of force, pain, coercion, or high levels of distress, it is *not* common for young children to exhibit aggressive or excessive sexual behaviors imitative of adult sexual activity (e.g., oral and anal sex, penetration). These warrant further evaluation.

- Explore alternate explanations for sexualized knowledge or behavior, such as the following:

  - overstimulation or confusion due to exposure to pornography while surfing the Internet, or watching videogames or cable TV
  - living in an overcrowded home, a home with little privacy, or a sexualized environment (e.g., witnessing sexual activity by babysitter, living with adults who engage in sexual activities after drug or alcohol use)

Table 9.1 provides a sampling of questions that explore a few of these issues.

Exploring Allegations of Physical Abuse

In suspicions of physical abuse, you may want to explore the following list of topics. Tables 9.2 and 9.3 present a sampling of questions that illustrate how to explore some of these topics in a developmentally sensitive fashion.

- How current physical injuries occurred (e.g., bruises, bleeding, cuts, fractures):

  - firsthand accounts of pain
  - subsequent medical treatments (bandaging, aspirin, visit to doctor)
  - use of weapons, verbal threats, type of force

Table 9.2 Sample Questions in Cases of Physical Abuse

■ **To elicit caretaker preferences, dislikes, and worries:**

Who takes care of you?...most of the time?...after school?...weekends? Who do you like to babysit/take care of you? Why? What do you do together? Who do you not like to take care of you? Why? What happens? What do you usually do together? What do you like best about [*caretakers listed*] taking care of you? What are the things you do not like about [*caretakers listed*] taking care of you? You said you hurt your ankle—who was watching you when it happened? Tell me more about how it happened. What did [*caretaker's name*] do/say when it happened? Do you worry about not being safe? When? Who is taking care of you when you worry? What do you worry might happen? What makes you think so? Do you feel safe when [*caretaker's name*] takes care of you? Why not? What might happen? What do you worry about happening? What makes you worry about that?

■ **Once a suspicious injury or event is reported, to inquire about the incident:**

What happened? What did [*caretaker's name*] do with his/her hands? What did [*caretaker's name*] say to you? Was anyone else in the room? Does anyone else know what happened? What happened right before it started?...after, when it was over? What else was going on at the time? Where were your brother/sister/other parent/other relatives? When did it happen? Daytime? Nighttime? Where did it happen? In the house, which room? Outside? What else happened that day? Why do you think it happened? What makes you think so? How did you feel? What did that feel like? What made you feel that way?

■ **Inquire about other incidents of abuse:**

Did something like this happen one time or more than one time? another time? What happened? Did something like this happen to someone else? Who? Did someone get hurt? Did [*person identified*] cry? Who went to get help? Did you go to a doctor for help/medicine? Are you worried it will happen again to you? Are you worried it will happen to someone else? Who? Did it happen one time or more than one time? Tell me about the other times. What was the first time? Last time? How was the other time not the same/different from this time? Have you seen the same thing happen to someone else? Have you seen someone else get hurt when [*caretaker name*] was taking care of you?

■ **Inquire about other witnesses/victims:**

Were there any other grownups there? Other children there? Who was in the room? Did [*person named*] see/hear what happened? What makes you think [*person named*] saw/heard what happened? What did the other children/adults do? Did you tell anyone about what happened? Who? What did [*person named*] say/do? What did you tell [*person named*]? What words did you use? Are you worried someone else is going to get hurt? Who? Why?

■ **Ask about family functioning and discipline:**

How is your family getting along? What kinds of things do you do together as a family? Any special activities or traditions? What happens on holidays in your family? What are some of the rules in your family for good behavior?...rules to keep everyone safe? What happens when children don't follow the rules?...don't listen?...don't do what they are supposed to do? Do they get punished? How? What do parents say/do when children are punished? Is there much yelling or hitting? What happens? What makes people in your family happy/yell/cry? Are some people in your family unhappy/sad/mad a lot? About what? What do people in your family yell about? Cry about? What makes them feel bad? Have things changed since you told what happened? Are you worried that someone will be angry with you? Hurt you again? What makes you worried about that?

Table 9.3 Sample Questions About Coercion and Force

- What would happen if you did not do what the grownup told you to do?

- Did the grownup tell/ask/make you do something you did not like/that hurt/scared you? What did the grownup do?

- Which body part(s) did the grownup use? What happened next? How did he/she make you do it? What words did he/she use?

- What did the grownup say would happen if you did not do what he told you to do?

- You said you couldn't get out of bed—why not? What was stopping you? You said he was holding you, how was he holding you? What was he doing with his hands?

- What do you think the grownup would do if you screamed/ran away?

- Did the grownup say something good would happen if you did what he said? What (privileges, rewards)?

- Did the grownup say something bad would happen if you didn't? What?

- Did the grownup warn/tell you not to tell anyone? To keep a secret? What did he say? Would someone be mad/hurt/sad if you talk about what happened?

- Was there hitting or pushing? Did anyone get hurt? Who? How?

- Were there bruises/marks on your skin afterwards? What did they look like? Were there body parts that were red or sore? Bruised or cut? What body parts got hurt?

- Whereabouts of other caretakers, siblings, relatives when injury occurred

- Efforts to keep injury a secret; what would happen if secret got out

- Ongoing medical conditions the child has been treated for (e.g., *What kinds of things do you go to doctor for? Take medicine for? Is there a problem you go to the doctor for a lot? What does the doctor do?*)

- Explanations for why injury occurred; explanations for similar previous injuries:

  - Whether a child believes an injury was intentional or unintentional (e.g., *Was it on purpose? By accident? How do you know he meant to hurt you? What did he say when he did it? Were you surprised he hurt you? Why weren't you surprised?*)
  - Child's reasons for use of force (discipline, punishment) to put conflicting explanations for injury in context (e.g., whether caretakers have substance abuse or explosive disorder)

- Evidence of incidents of violence by the alleged offender toward others (e.g., *Did you see the same* (or *almost the same*) *thing happen to someone else? What happened? Who was there? What did they do or say?*)

- Discipline and rule violations in the home:

  - Ask children for a list of rules for good behavior at home (e.g., *Be polite, Clean up your mess, Don't talk back, Don't run into street, Don't steal or lie*)
  - Ask what happens when children don't follow the rules in their family (e.g., *What happens when a child in your house does not follow the rules? What if someone does not clean up her mess?...does not tell the truth? Does not listen to her parents?*) and how caretakers react (*What does your mom do/say when that happens?*)
  - Ask how parents enforce the rules
  - Ask what makes caretakers happy/sad/angry

Tables 9.2 and 9.3 display samplings of questions phrased in a developmentally sensitive fashion about physical abuse, coercion, and force.

Exploring Allegations of Neglect, Failure to Protect, and Lack of Supervision

With allegations of neglect, details revolve around the quality of care children receive, with sensitivity to issues of poverty, lack of education, caretaker substance-use, or parental mental illness. It is important to remember that children may feel ambivalent about revealing disparaging household facts that can be embarrassing or shameful. Hence, interviewers need to maintain an unbiased, nonjudgmental stance towards the caretakers and the allegations. Remember that most caretakers have as many or more moments of positive than negative caretaking, and children will appreciate your objectivity when you explore these as well (e.g., Child: "One time on my birthday we had cake and presents. It was fun." Interviewer: "Sounds like you had fun with your mom that day. Tell me more about that time."). A child who has been neglected for a long time may perceive that her care was adequate. Ask for descriptions of specific events using the event categories, not evaluative comments

Table 9.4 Sample Questions About Substance Use in Caretakers

- Tell me who takes care of you—at home? After school? At night? Are you worried about any of these people? Does this person have a problem that scares/worries you? Why? Are you worried someone will get hurt? Are there times you feel not safe? Tell me about those times.

- Does your mom/dad/babysitter eat or drink or smoke anything that makes them act funny? What happens? Do you feel scared something bad might happen after they do it? What could happen? Do you have some worries about your mom/dad/babysitter? What kinds of things worry you? Do you worry a grownup in your house might get hurt? What might happen?

- Do you think one of the adults you know has a problem with drinking beer or wine, with taking drugs or smoking? Who? What makes you think it is a problem?

- Did you hear someone tell your mom she should try to stop? Did your mom say she wanted to stop?

- Did the adult get into trouble after she did it? Get hurt? Fall down? Get into a car accident? Go to the hospital or a doctor because of the problem? Are you worried they might get in trouble? Why?

- Who have you told about the problem? Who else knows? How did they learn about it?

- Does your mom/dad/babysitter need to get help for the problem? What makes you think so? Is there something you saw or heard that makes you think a grownup in the family has a problem? What? Is there anyone else who could tell me more about the problem?

(e.g., "You said you missed a lot of school? Why was that? Why couldn't she get up to take you? What stopped her? What made you late that day?"). In addition, Table 9.4 displays a sampling of questions that explore caretakers' use of alcohol and drugs. In allegations of neglect or lack of supervision, you may want to help children elaborate details in the areas that follow.

Household Organization

To determine the extent of household chaos or structure, ask the child to recount a usual day in the household (e.g. "Tell me what happens in your house from the time you get up until the time you go to bed"). Prompt children to tell what happens right before and right after events so they do not skip large gaps in the day (e.g., Interviewer: "What happens right before you get in the car to drive to school?" Child: "I get dressed and have breakfast first."). Explore the following:

- routines and schedules

- who wakes children up for school, monitors dressing, keeps track of time, etc.

- who encourages self-care activities, such as teeth-brushing

- who monitors homework

- who provides transportation to school

- whether the whole family sits down together for meals

- who prepares meals and whether children prepare their own food

Hygiene

Explore whether the child has adequate hygiene, including the following:

- whether the child bathes and brushes teeth regularly

- whether shampoo and soap are available

- whether clothes are washed regularly

- whether the child thinks her clothes fit and how she gets new ones when they get too small

- whether the child has been instructed on how to stay healthy

- whether the child has been rejected by peers for unkempt appearance

Nutrition

Explore whether the child has adequate nutrition, including the following:

- whether the child gets enough to eat at home

- whether she is sent to school with adequate provisions

- whether the child understands what kinds of foods are healthy

- whether the child has gone for long periods without food

Safety

Explore children's perceptions of household rules around safety (*What are the rules in your house for keeping everyone safe?*) and consequences for violations of safety rules (*What happens when someone doesn't follow the rules?*):

- Note the child's fears or worries about what could go wrong and make her not safe.

- If the child mentions that caretakers are upset, explore what they do when upset and how caretakers calm themselves down when upset (e.g., withdraw, yell, take pills, drink a beer).

Supervision

Explore issues of supervision, including the following:

- whether the child is left alone or outside the home, and the circumstances for doing so

- whether the child is ever left overnight without adult presence or in the care of strangers

- whether the child has hurt himself while unsupervised, and who intervened (neighbors, relatives)

- whether the child has been told to do things he thinks he should not be doing or would get him in trouble with the police

Cleanliness

Explore the cleanliness of the child's environment. Ask her who cleans the house and for descriptions of specific actions (e.g., *Who cleans your house? What does she do to clean up a mess? What happens to the dirty dishes? Who cleans the clothes? Who throws out garbage?).*

Education

Explore caretaking related to the child's education, including the following:

- whether child receives help with homework when needed

- whether the child receives timely transportation to school

- whether the child has sufficient school supplies

- whether the parents communicate with teachers

Medical Care

Explore how responsive caretakers are when children are ill or injured (*Who takes care of you when you are sick? What does he do to help you feel better? What happens when a child in your family is sick? Needs medicine? Did you go to the doctor? What happened? What did your dad do? Say? What happens when someone throws up?*). Ask if children go to doctor or dentist for checkups or whether they have any ongoing problems that require continuous or repeated medical care.

Social Development

Explore whether children have been allowed/encouraged to participate in friendships or social activities outside the home (*Do you have friends? What are their names? Which are your best friends? Do you visit their homes? What do you do there? Do they visit your house? What happens when friends come to your house to play?*). Explore the reasons why children may have few friends or do not want to bring their friends home or to meet their family. Explore whether grownups act in ways that are unusual or that might scare friends, or if there are reasons why friends might tease them.

Conclusion

The goal of this chapter is to acquaint readers with the process of formulating developmentally sensitive questions about what children have seen, heard, felt, and understood when there are suspicions of child abuse or neglect. The chapter provides a list of topics commonly addressed when there are allegations of sexual abuse, physical abuse, neglect, and lack of supervision. The tables in this chapter provide some sample language for formulating questions to explore these topics.

Phase III Closure

Chapter 10   *Closing the Interview*[1]

Materials

- Index cards (optional)
- Business cards (optional)

Outline

- Warn the child that the interview is winding down
- Summarize the key points the child has communicated
- Give the child a chance to ask questions and express his/her feelings
- Educate the child about the next step(s) in the process
- Dispel fears but avoid false promises
- Give the child time to regain composure if needed
- Bolster child's perspective and sense of mastery
- Plan positive strategies for coping
- Assess whether referrals are necessary
- Check for safety issues

Introduction

Phase III of the DNE interview focuses on terminating the interview with developmental sensitivity—in a way that leaves children more likely to engage openly and honestly in subsequent interviews or in courtroom testimony. Failing to budget time for closure and abruptly dismissing children with brief comments like "Thanks for coming in; we will be in touch" or "You can go to the waiting room now; I want to talk to your mom" may impair their cooperation and motivation at subsequent stages of the forensic process.

Warning Children That the Interview Is Winding Down

By this point, you have, at a minimum, provided an opportunity for the child to tell you what is important to him. Whether or not the subsequent interview elicits descriptions of any incidents of forensic relevance, five or 10 minutes before the end, inform the child that you are almost finished and tell him how many minutes remain. For children under second grade, you can point to the hands on a clock or set a timer.

Watch closely how the child responds. Is he relieved? Does he become provocative and angry? Is he anxious about separating or worried about the impending or imagined consequences if incidents of suspected abuse or neglect have been discussed in the interview? These may be clues to his ability or inability to cope with the thoughts and feelings that have been stirred up, in cases of both genuine victimization as well as coaching or false allegation.

Throughout the interview, you need to pay attention to children's communications about when they have had enough. They "speak" with their behavior (e.g., restless, fidgety, increasing frustration and anger) and their words ("Are we done yet?"; "I want to see my mom now"; "Can I play with those toys over there?"; "Can I go now?"). Acknowledge rather than ignore these signals ("I see you are ready to go, so let's start to finish. We will be done in a few minutes").

You may want to use the last few minutes to summarize what you have learned about what is important to the child. Consider the following sample summary:

> *You have told me you are worried about going back home and whether your mom will take drugs or hurt herself. You have told me that sometimes your stepdad drinks a lot of beers and then he gets mad. When that happens, he yells and sometimes he hits you, your mom, and your brother. One time, your mom took you and your brother to your aunt's house so you wouldn't get hurt again. You have told me you really like baseball and you don't want to lose the team if your parents get divorced and you have to move.*

As always, invite the child to correct you:

- *Did I get this right?*

- *Am I understanding you correctly?*

Even when children say very little of forensic relevance, you can still summarize what you have observed. For example, one study described a child who was silent but repeatedly punched a doll after taking off the doll's clothing. The interviewer merely commented, "Punching and taking off clothes seem to be very important to you." This leaves the door open for a second interview.

Suggesting a Second Meeting

You can give your business card to the child and caregiver and suggest another meeting instead of pressuring children or resorting to leading or high-pressure techniques. For example:

- *If you want to talk again, you or your mom can call me at the number on this card.*

- *Let's set up another time to talk together one more time.*

During this phase, offer the child an opportunity to have his questions answered. For example:

- *You have told me a lot. Is there anything you want to ask me now?*

- *Is there anything I can tell you?*

- *Is there something else you want to know/learn?*

Sometimes children's questions reveal gaps in knowledge that are easily addressed. Sometimes their questions raise profound issues about their families, bodies, or the consequences of the interview that you don't know the answers to. When this occurs, tell the child his questions are important. Make a list on an index card of his questions to ask parents or attorneys later. You may wish to say something like the following:

- *I don't know the answer to that, but let's ask your attorney. Let's make a list of questions to ask him later so we don't forget.*

Questions About the Aftermath of the Interview

If children ask questions about the aftermath of the interview, such as, "They aren't going to put my mom/dad in jail, are they?" you can respond by saying something like the following:

> *I don't really know what will happen next. And I don't want to tell you something that is not true. That wouldn't be fair to you. So we will talk to the adults who are making the decisions and find out what will happen next as soon as we can. What I do know is that we are working on making sure you stay safe and healthy, that no one gets hurt.*

Personal Questions

Children often ask personal questions about you ("Do you have kids? Can you take me home?") or about your trauma history ("Did your daddy make you suck his dick?"). Rather than personal disclosure, you can respond to the underlying message of the question, which is "Am I the only one this has ever happened to? Do you think I am weird? Do you understand why this happened?" In your comments, acknowledge the child's concerns and, if appropriate, tell him you are going to set up a talk with a mental health professional. You can say the following:

> *I have talked to a lot of people about their lives and their problems. Everyone, including me, has had things happen that they did not like or things that were upsetting. If you want to talk more about your feelings, I will find someone for you to talk to. I know a grownup whose job is to talk to kids about their feelings, problems, and worries.*

Interview Impressions

This can be a time to check out older children's impressions of the interview. This is helpful if you plan another interview. Sample questions include the following:

- *I am curious about how the interview went for you. Was it the same as you expected it to be?... different than you expected? In what way?*

- *What did you find difficult about the interview?*

- *What might have made it easier for you?*

Concluding Interviews with Children Who Report Victimization, Neglect, or Threats

When children report maltreatment during the interview, you may want to consider the following during the closure phase:

- Acknowledge that something important was said without stating whether you agree or disagree with its accuracy or veracity: *What you have told me is very important.*

- Find out the child's fears of or worries about the consequences of their disclosure:

  - *Is there anything else you want to tell me? Ask me?*
  - *Do you think something will change after today? What? Why?*

- *How will you feel about that change? Will that be a good change? Why? Will you be happy/sad about that change? What will make you feel that way? Why will you feel different after our talk today? Are you scared/worried something might change after today? What are you scared/worried about?*
- *Do you think anyone else will be happy that you talked to me today? Who? Why?*
- *Are you worried anyone will not be happy with you for talking to me today? Who? Why?*

- Make sure the child feels safe to report future incidents of abuse/ threat or instances of retaliation:

  - *What can we do to make sure no one gets hurt again?*
  - *What would you do if something like this started to happen again?*
  - *Is there a safe place you could go? Where?*
  - *Who would you tell? Could you tell your* [non-offending] *parent, grandparent? aunt? babysitter? teacher? neighbor?*

- Find out if the child wants anyone else to know what was said:

  - *Are there any grownups I should talk to about this?*
  - *Who else needs to know to keep you safe?*

- Find out if the child has been coached to deny or confabulate:

  - *Who told you that you were coming here today? What did he say about it? What did he say about how to answer the questions?*
  - *What were you told about talking to me today?*
  - *Did someone tell you what to say or what not to say?*

- Ask if the child has been threatened:

  - *Is there something else about what happened that you do not want to tell me right now?*
  - *Did someone tell you not to talk to me? Who? What did they say?*
  - *Did someone tell you to talk with me today? Who? What did they say?*
  - *Did someone say good/bad things would happen if you did? Who? What did they say?*
  - *What might happen if you tell me any more about what happened?*

- Give the child an opportunity to talk to you or someone else about what happened in the future:

  - *Do you want to talk to me again?*
  - *Do you think there might be more to talk about another time?*

- Offer the opportunity to be referred to a counselor:

  - *Sometimes talking about these things makes you have a lot of feelings. I know someone whose job is to help kids with problems and who tries to help them with their feelings.*

Educating Children About the Next Steps in the Process

Facing the unknown is anxiety-provoking for anyone. In particular, children typically lack basic information and may fill in the gaps with fear or misinformation. To decrease their anxiety about the future, prepare children for the next few steps to the extent that you know what they are. Will they be talking to a social worker or attorney? Will a judge be making a decision about their family?

Preparing a child for trial is beyond the scope of this book; however, you can tell the young child who asks about going to trial the following information, which is drawn from our studies of preparing children for court (Nathanson & Saywitz, 2003; Saywitz, 1989; Saywitz, et al., 1990; Saywitz & Nathanson, 1993a & 1993b).

- Going to trial will involve a special meeting in a courtroom (a picture of a courtroom depicting the judge, witness, jury, and attorneys at tables can be a useful tool).

- The person who is in charge of the meeting is called the Judge. The judge's job is to make sure everything is safe and fair.

- People who have important information (witnesses) are called to the courtroom to answer questions about what they saw or heard.

- Two separate teams of people, sometimes called lawyers or attorneys, will ask the questions so everyone can hear all the facts/ information important to each side of the story.

Sometimes children express reluctance to repeat their statements in court (e.g., "I already told my therapist and my teacher. Ask them."). In such cases you can explain that the attorneys will ask questions during the meeting in the courtroom so the judge and the people who help the judge decide what happens next (the jury) can hear the information for themselves.

Dispelling Fears but Avoiding False Promises

Children experience numerous fears born out of ignorance, misperception, threats of reprisal or out-of-home placement, as well as fears of abandonment, adult rejection/anger, or loss of love. Even when children know that someone has been arrested, they harbor fears due to ignorance (e.g., "People in jail escape when the police go home at night."). You can show you understand and accept children's concerns and perspectives without leading, taking sides, or endorsing a particular version of what happened. When children express fears, you can

- offer knowledge and reassurance when possible;

- allow children to raise fears they have about their case (e.g., "Is the social worker going to take me?") rather than devalue or minimize their concerns (e.g., "Don't be worried.");

- normalize their fears when reasonable (e.g., "Most people feel worried if they do not know what will happen next.");

- suggest things children can do when they feel scared or worried, like identify an adult they can talk to, or use the positive strategies for coping described later in this chapter;

- ask what kinds of things the child does at home to calm himself down when he gets upset/worried/scared/mad (e.g., talk to someone, listen to music, play basketball, draw); and

- offer to help find out answers to concerns within the parameters of your role.

Refrain from making false promises outside of your control ("Your mom will understand."; "He's not going to jail."; "Everything will be okay."). Instead, try to set up a meeting among yourself, the child, and the appropriate adult.

Giving Children Time to Regain Their Composure

If a child becomes upset during an interview, don't respond too quickly with support and structure. It can give the impression that you cannot tolerate or do not want to hear what really happened or how deep the child's emotions run. If you become uncomfortable, wait a few moments, quietly observing the child—children often are relieved to meet someone who is not afraid to hear about something that has frightened them.

Once the child has described the event in sufficient detail, you can begin to move away from the upsetting topic, using the following strategies:

- Thank the child for her cooperation and motivation (two capacities not to be taken for granted).

- Acknowledge any earlier demonstrations of avoidance, frustration, ambivalence, or sadness. Consider saying something like the following:

  - *In the beginning you told me it was hard for you to talk to me. Thank you for trying hard even though it was not easy for you.*
  - *In the beginning you said you were very sad. Thank you for staying in here with me and trying your best.*

- Normalize the pattern of rising and falling emotion—becoming upset and calming down: *Everyone gets upset sometimes. And then they figure out how to calm themselves down.*

- When appropriate, model strategies for calming down (e.g., deep breathing—*When people get upset or worried, sometimes they find it helps to take a slow deep breath, like this. Let's try it together.*), self-soothing (e.g., self-talk) and stress reduction (e.g., muscle relaxation).

Helping Children Gain Perspective and Consolidate from a Position of Mastery

Give every child the impression he has completed the interview successfully, regardless of the content of the discussion. You want to leave the child with the impression that he has made a contribution to the process, and his statements and preferences are heard. At the same time, you need to refrain from giving the sense that you agree or disagree with the child's point of view or that the child's preferences or wishes will be fulfilled (e.g., to live with one parent over another; to go to Grandmother's house instead of into foster care). If the child has revealed a shameful or painful event, his sense of dignity and self-esteem is, in part, a function of how he sees himself in your eyes. Your reaction to what was said or not said in the interview can influence his willingness to participate in future steps (e.g., if the interviewer shows he is disappointed that more was not revealed). After one interview, a child told her mom, "I can't believe I told him all those disgusting things Mr. Jones did to me. He's gonna think I'm awful. I never want to see him again."

Bolster the Child's Sense of Self-Efficacy

Phrase your comments in terms of capability and adeptness, avoiding remarks related to the facts of the case so as to avoid biasing future statements. You may wish to say something like this:

> *You took this interview seriously, and that will help me to do my job. Thank you.*

Compliment the Child's Handling of the Interview

Comment on how well the child has coped with the demands of the interview. This can be a brief summary statement about the interview process itself, reviewing how well the child cooperated, listened, and remembered despite conflicting feelings. For example:

> *Some of the questions I asked you were easy to answer, but maybe some were hard to answer. Thank you for working hard to do your best to listen and answer.*

Reframe Fear as Bravery

Reframe children's comments indicating they are fearful or worried as being brave despite their fears and worries. Children often define "bravery" as doing something in the absence of scary feelings; redefine it as participating in the interview *despite* scary feelings. For example:

> *You told me you were scared to talk about this. It was very brave of you to talk with me even though you were scared.*

Phrase Comments in a Positive Way

Children who have been victims of an unpredictable adult world (e.g., abuse, neglect, divorce, accident, violence) can be very controlling in the interview, telling you what to do and what not to do; changing or avoiding the topic. The interview requires children to follow your agenda, which flies in the face of their best way of coping with anxiety—avoidance. To reduce tension, avoid negative phrasing. Instead of saying, "You don't like to be helpless," or "You need to be in control," phrase comments in a positive way, such as "I noticed that you like to take charge of things, to be on top of things."

Planning Positive Strategies for Coping

Help Children Anticipate How They Will Feel Later

Ask children to anticipate their thoughts and feelings after they leave the interview. Ask them how they might feel later. If children express fear or worry during the interview, you might say:

> *When we first met, you said you did not want to talk about these things because it makes you sad and scared. How will you feel later today once you leave?*

Generate a List of Coping Strategies

When children anticipate negative reactions, help them generate a list of anticipatory coping strategies they can use at home.

- If children anticipate future negative affect states, identify coping strategies; e.g., *Let's think of some things you can do at home to make yourself feel better—talk to your sister, listen to music, write a letter to your mom.*

■ If children cannot think of anything, ask what they usually do to calm down or comfort themselves when they get upset. Query them about a specific time and what made them feel better.

■ The list should include identifying a safe adult to contact and deciding how the contact would occur, as well as notifying the adult that the child plans to contact him in case of emotional distress.

■ Give children a note card to take home with the list of strategies written down.

Assess Whether Referrals Are Needed

It is difficult to predict who will be faced with an onslaught of painful, frightening images when they return to the neighborhood where an assault or kidnapping took place. You cannot predict who will feel overcome with regret when disclosure of abuse leads to out-of-home placement, or who will run away or engage in self-destructive or aggressive behavior. But if the child is vulnerable, with several risk factors and few protective factors, she should be evaluated briefly for referral to a mental health professional before leaving the interview. Some of the following risk factors can help to identify vulnerable children in need of greater attention:

■ weak support system

■ limited or no access to mental health resources

■ history of post-traumatic distress

■ history of depression

■ history of self-injurious behavior

■ history of running away from home

■ evidence of drug or alcohol use

■ impulse-control problems

■ history of aggressive outbursts

Table 10.1 Signs of Childhood Depression

- Depressed, sad, or irritable mood most of the day, nearly every day (e.g., tearful)

- Loss of interest or pleasure in activities that used to bring the child pleasure, most of the day, nearly every day

- Socially withdrawn, not talkative, poor eye contact, indifferent

- Fatigue or loss of energy most of the day, nearly every day

- Poor appetite, weight loss, or failure to make expected weight gains

- Feelings of worthlessness, hopelessness, excessive guilt, even self-hatred and self-flagellation

- Difficulty concentrating and making decisions, nearly every day

- Difficulty sleeping or sleeping too much during the day

- Recurrent thoughts of death or suicide

- Long latencies before responding to others

Adapted from American Psychiatric Association (2000), *Diagnostic and Statistical Manual of Mental Disorders* (4th ed., text rev., pp. 369–376).

For example, childhood depression is not uncommon in child victims of crime. One study found abused children to be four times as likely to have suffered from a depressive disorder as are non-abused children (Lanktree, Briere, & Zaidi, 1991). Hence, children who appear withdrawn, dysphoric, tearful, hopeless, helpless, self-denigrating, and who fail to make eye contact, should be assessed a little further for signs of depression. Table 10.1 lists common symptoms of childhood depression. Similarly, Table 10.2 lists common symptoms of post-traumatic distress.

When children have a history of maladaptive coping patterns in the past or exhibit signs of substantial distress in the present, let the child know you are finished with questions about what happened, but you were wondering about something else. Then assess the need for further evaluation and referral; if you are a mental health professional, consider whether it is within your role to conduct an evaluation or to refer the child to another professional. If you do not feel qualified to make such inquires but have concerns, make the appropriate referral to a professional.

At a minimum, you can ask the child:

- how he is feeling now that the interview is over,

- if he feels he wants or will need some help with something,

Table 10.2 Signs of Post-Traumatic Distress

When children have been exposed to a situation that they perceive as threatening them with death or injury and that evokes a response of intense fear, they may respond with disorganized, agitated behavior, including the following three types of signs:

- Re-experiencing the traumatic event;
- Persistent avoidance of stimuli associated with event; and
- Persistent symptoms of increased arousal.

Event Re-experienced:

- Intrusive, distressing recollections of the event in the form of images, thoughts, and/or perceptions (e.g., recurrent nightmares)
- Repetitive-preoccupied play containing themes or aspects of the traumatic event
- Flashbacks, dissociative episodes, re-enactments, acting/feeling as if the event were recurring
- Intense distress at exposure to internal or external cues that remind or symbolize the traumatic event
- Physiological reactivity (e.g., increased heart rate, difficulty breathing) and/or anxiety at reminders

Avoidance:

- Avoidance of thoughts, feelings, and/or conversations associated with trauma (can include interview)
- Avoidance of activities, places, and/or people that are reminders of the trauma (can include interviewer)
- Lack of recall of an important aspect of trauma
- Diminished interest or participation in significant activities
- Lowered motivation, decreased cooperation, indifference
- Feelings of detachment or estrangement from others
- Restricted range of affect

Increased Arousal:

- Difficulty falling and/or staying asleep
- Irritability or anger outbursts
- Difficulty concentrating
- Hypervigilance, safety concerns
- Exaggerated startle response

Adapted from American Psychiatric Association (2000), *Diagnostic and Statistical Manual of Mental Disorders* (4th ed., text rev., pp. 436–468).

- if he wishes something were different than it is, or

- if he wants to talk with someone else about his feelings or problems.

Check for Safety Issues

Certain mental health problems, not uncommon in a population of child victim/witnesses, involve symptoms that can be dangerous to the child or to others. At the very least, concerns such as the following should not be ignored:

- suicidal ideation

- extreme risk-taking behaviors

- running away

- drug and alcohol use

- self-destructive behavior (e.g., cutting)

- violence toward others

Our point here is that children's mental health concerns are not always obvious. Consider safety issues before returning children to caretakers, relatives, social services, or law-enforcement personnel at the close of the interview. If you have concerns, be sure the child will be well monitored by adults and, when necessary, connected to the appropriate referrals in a timely fashion.

Conclusion

In summary, Phase III, Closure, is a time of transition from the interview to the outside world where all the real and perceived consequences and complications are waiting. Your goal is to help children feel they have made a positive contribution to the process and successfully completed the interview, regardless of the content of discussion. Your goal is to take the time to review key points, give children a chance to ask questions and express feelings, dispel fears when possible, educate them about next steps, anticipate problems and identify anticipatory coping strategies, assess whether referrals are necessary, and check for safety concerns. When children have reported upsetting events, give them time for re-composure; help them understand that their memories, thoughts, feelings, and preferences have been heard; and find out whether they have fears or worries about what might happen as a consequence of their statements. After working so hard to develop rapport and create a developmentally sensitive experience, take care to devote the last five to 10 minutes to these activities to promote the child's motivation, cooperation, and performance in future interviews or courtroom testimony.

Appendices

Appendix A   *Reminder Cards for Elementary School–Aged Children*

This page may be photocopied and the individual cards can be cut out for use.

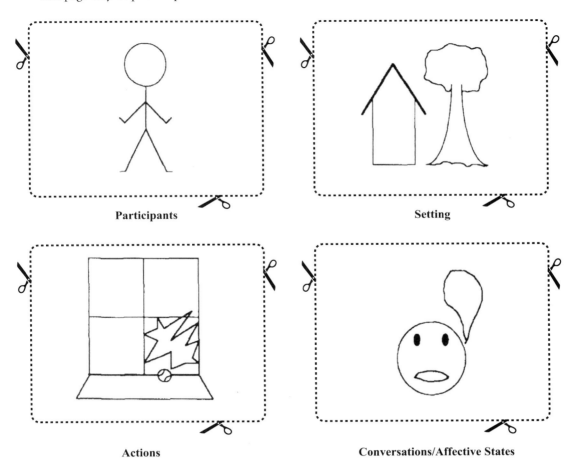

Participants

Setting

Actions

Conversations/Affective States

Reprinted from Saywitz, K. J. & Snyder, L. (1996). Narrative Elaboration: Test of a new procedure for interviewing children. *Journal of Consulting and Clinical Psychology, 64*, 1347–1357.

Appendix B *Reminders Cards for Preschoolers*

This page may be photocopied and the individual cards can be cut out for use.

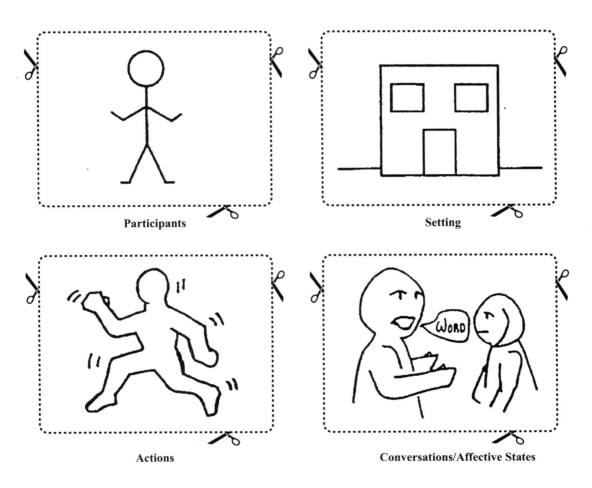

Participants

Setting

Actions

Conversations/Affective States

From Dorado, J. S. & Saywitz, K. J. (2001). Interviewing preschoolers from low- and middle-SES communities: A test of the Narrative Elaboration recall improvement technique. *Journal of Clinical Child Psychology, 30,* 568–580. Reprinted with kind permission of Taylor & Francis, Ltd., http://www.informaworld.com.

Appendix C *Sample Transcript of Child Learning to Use the Reminder Cards*

INTERVIEWER: If you were going to tell someone about what you did with me today, what would you tell them?

CHILD'S FREE RECALL REPORT: We went to the office. We talked. [Is that all?] Yes.

INTERVIEWER: Good. Now let's use the reminder cards to tell more about what happened. See this card? This is the *People Card.* When you tell about the things that have happened, this card reminds you to tell about all the people who were there and how each person looked—you could tell the names of all the people that were there and what they looked like or how they were dressed. Let's use it now. [Interviewer places card in front of child.] If you were going to tell someone all about what we did, you would tell them about all the people you met here, like me and what I looked like, and my name. Let's practice now. What would you tell them about me?

CHILD'S ELABORATION: You have long hair. Blackish brown. [Anything else?] You have those beads on your wrist. [Good job! There might be more things you could tell if you remembered. You could tell them I was an adult. And this card could remind you to tell what clothes I have on, too.] You have a dress. [Good job. You could tell my name if you remembered it.] I don't know. [Great job. You only told what you remembered. So what does this card remind you to tell?] About the people. [And what they looked like. Great. Let's try another card.]

INTERVIEWER: See this card? This is the *Places Card.* It reminds you to tell where something happened—where it was and how the place looked. You could tell if it happened inside or outside. If it happened inside, you could tell which room and all about what the room looked like. Let's use it now. If you were going to tell someone where we worked today and what it looked like, what would you tell them?

CHILD'S ELABORATION: We went to Mrs. Balick's office. We went down the hall by the cafeteria. [Good job, you remembered a lot. There might be more things you could tell if you remembered them. You could also tell about the furniture in the room or the pictures on the wall. Some of the little things in the room. Let's practice now. What else could you tell about the place?] We went to the office. (*Looks around the room a bit.*) There's a computer and desk. A picture of Cinderella on the wall. [Great. That's a lot. If you remember, you could tell about the windows and what you can see outside. Anything else you can tell about the place?] Yeah, out the window, there's the playground with the swings and slide. The Seastars class is out there playing now. [Good. Now what does this card remind you to tell?] Where it happened. [Great, and what it looked like. Let's practice with the next card.]

INTERVIEWER: This is the *What Happened Card.* [Holds up card.] It reminds you to tell what happened, what the people did—all the things that happened and as much as you can about what people did. Let's use it now. [Places card in front of child.] So what happened here in the office?

CHILD'S ELABORATION: You mean you are showing me these cards? [Yes. What else did we do?] You lost your pen and looked for it. [I did. What else?] Talking about the room. [Yes, and if you remembered, you could say that I asked you questions, you could tell about the camera we set up to make a video recording.] Oh yeah, you couldn't get it to work right and so you got that guy to help you with the tape and the camera when Ms. Balick came back in to get some papers. The guy was tall. He said his name, but I can't remember now. [Great, you told so much more about what happened this morning, but only what you remembered. You are learning fast. Let's practice with the last card.]

INTERVIEWER: This is the *Talking and Feeling Card.* It reminds you to tell about what people said and how they were feeling—what kinds of things people talked about, the words they used if you remember them, and how they were feeling. Let's use it now. [Places card in front of child.] If you were to tell someone what we said today, what would you tell them?

CHILD'S ELABORATION: You said we should practice using the cards to remember. You said you would take me back to my class after. You told Mrs. Balick to come in and get the papers. She said thank you. [Great job! You said that I lost my pen, how do you think I was feeling?] Sad. [What makes you think I was sad?] You said it was your favorite. Someone gave it to you for your birthday. You said you were sad if you lost it. [Good job telling me what I said. If you remember, you could tell that I was happy when I found it. Do you think I was happy?] Yes. [What made you think so?] You smiled. You said you were happy. [You told me a lot about what I said. What about some of the things that you said?] Oh. Okay, when we were walking, too? [Yes.] I told you I like art and soccer and to draw. [Great job. You are really trying hard to tell as much as you remember. Now, what do we use this card for?] To tell what we talked about. [Yes, to tell what the people said and how they were feeling: good job!]

INTERVIEWER SUMMARY: You used the cards and you remembered a lot. You learned you can remember the parts of what happened and tell about it better when you use the reminder cards. [Holds up *People Card*]. The People Card reminds you to tell who was there and how each person looked. [Holds up the *Places Card*.] The Places Card reminds you to tell where it was and how the place looked. [Holds up the *What Happened Card*.] The What Happened Card reminds you to tell what happened and what the people did. [Holds up the *Talking and Feeling Card*.]. And the Talking and Feeling card reminds you to tell what people said and how they felt. Also, you learned that it is important to tell as much as you can remember, even the little things, but don't guess or make anything up.

Appendix D *Sample Transcript of Additional Practice Task*

Transcript of Preschooler Practicing Recall of Morning Routine Using Reminder Cards

INTERVIEWER: Tell me what happened this morning from the time you got up until the time you came here.

CHILD'S FREE RECALL: (*Thinks for a long time*) I was asleep [mm hm]. Then I waked up [mm hm], then I waked up [mm hm], then I had breakfast, then I went to school.

INTERVIEWER—LEARNING CUED ELABORATION: Let's use the reminder cards.

INTERVIEWER—PEOPLE CARD: This is the People Card. It reminds you to tell who was there. Who was there this morning?

CHILD'S CUED ELABORATION—PEOPLE: Daddy. [Anyone else?] Mommy. [Anyone else?] Alia and me. [Who is Alia?] She my sister. [This card helps remind you to tell what the people looked like. What did the people look like?] My sister has curly hair, and I have curly hair, and mama has straight hair, and daddy has um (*pause*) he puts his hair in a ponytail. [It helps remind you to tell what kind of clothes the people were wearing, too. What clothes were the people wearing?] I don't know. [What did their bodies look like?] My mom's body is white and my sister's looks white; my body is brown and so is my dad's.

INTERVIEWER—WHAT HAPPENED CARD: This is the What Happened Card. It reminds you to tell what happened—what the people did this morning. Let's use it now. What did the people do this morning?

CHILD'S CUED ELABORATION—WHAT HAPPENED: My mom was like, she was making my lunch and I was getting dressed. [To tell more about what happened, you could tell what happened right before you got dressed.] My mom taked a shower and then she went to school, my sister was, uh (*pause*), I was making a card. [You said your sister was there, what was your sister doing?] She stopped to hit me. Alia gets in trouble sometimes. [You said you had breakfast, what did you have?] Cereal and milk.

INTERVIEWER—PLACES CARD: This is the Places Card. It reminds you to tell where you were, what the place looked like.

CHILD'S CUED ELABORATION—PLACES: I was at my house in my mama's room and my room. [What does your mama's room look like?] She has a bed and she has lots of white curtains. [This card can remind you to tell what is in the room, like any furniture.] My mom has drawers for her clothes.

INTERVIEWER—TALKING FEELING CARD: This is the Talking/Feeling Card. It reminds you to tell what the people said. What did people say this morning?

CHILD'S CUED ELABORATION—TALKING FEELING: My Mom said it's six o'clock and, um, go get dressed. [You said your daddy was there; did he say anything to you?] No, he said something to somebody else. [What did he say?] Uh, fix the alarm because I had the alarm last time. [You said your sister was there, did she say anything?] Yeah, hurry up, she has a test today. [How were the people feeling?] Happy. [What makes you think they were happy?] Because I saw it.

Note: *This child's free recall has about three chunks of unique information. She woke up, ate breakfast, and went to school. With cued elaboration, she provided an additional 23 pieces of information.*

Appendix E *Thinking Cards for Resisting Suggestive Questions*

This page may be photocopied and the individual cards can be cut out for use.

I don't know.

I don't remember.

No, that's wrong.

Yes, I know the answer

Saywitz, K. J. & Moan-Hardie, S. (1994). Reducing the potential for distortion of childhood memories. *Consciousness and Cognition, 3,* 408–425.

Artwork by Michael Dobrzycki.

Notes

Chapter 1

1. Those familiar with child development research will recognize our heavy reliance on Lev Vygotsky's work on the zone of proximal development.
2. Subsequent studies have included three-year-olds and demonstrated beneficial results, as described in Chapter 2.

Chapter 2

1. In the original studies, we used three mock-recall tasks (two videotaped vignettes and recall of what child and interviewer had done together so far). In subsequent studies, we used only one mock-recall task, eliminating the recall of the videotaped vignettes.
2. For the remainder of the guide, we use the term "open-ended recall" to refer to non-redundant information from free recall plus cued-elaboration recall.
3. Kulkofsky (2010) did find increases in the number of incorrect pieces of information but not in the proportion of errors. In addition, the vast majority of the errors she found were made by children with low vocabulary test scores, a group with a mean age of less than three and a half years.
4. Similar to previous research with the NE, standard deviations for children in both the NE and NE-no training groups were quite large. Re-examination of the data revealed two outliers. When these two outliers were removed from the data, the standard deviations were dramatically reduced.
5. Free recall for both interview conditions plus new descriptors reported during cued elaboration for the NE.

6. Total interview recall in NE condition: Descriptors reported in free recall plus cued elaboration recall plus in response to probed questions; Total interview recall in SP condition: Descriptors reported in free recall plus in response to probed questions. For both conditions, only unique descriptors (not previously reported) were coded.

7. Although Camparo and Camparo did find that children in the NE interview condition provided significantly more inaccurate descriptors in response to open-ended questions than did children in the standard-interview condition, this finding reflects the fact that the children in the standard-interview condition only rarely, if ever, used any descriptors of any sort to modify their reports. They used a mean of only 2.16 accurate descriptors and 0.00 inaccurate descriptors during their free recall, whereas children in the NE group used a mean of 15.62 accurate descriptors and only 2.24 inaccurate descriptors during their free-recall plus cued elaboration. Thus, proportionally speaking, children in the NE group spontaneously provided nearly seven times more accurate than inaccurate descriptors, whereas children in the standard protocol condition spontaneously provided only twice as many accurate as inaccurate descriptors.

8. However, the total number of descriptors about the fictitious event provided during free recall plus cued elaboration by children interviewed with the NE was significantly greater (mean = 2.28) than the total number of descriptors about the fictitious event provided during free recall only by children interviewed with the standard interview (mean = 0.05). Again, this finding can be explained by the fact that children in the standard protocol rarely, if ever, provided any descriptors at all in free recall.

9. *Learning disabilities* refers to "a disorder in one or more of the basic psychological processes involved in understanding or using spoken or written language which is not primarily the result of a visual, hearing, or motor impairment, mental retardation, serious emotional disturbance, or an environmental, cultural, or economic disadvantage.... The disorder includes without limitations, such conditions as perceptual disabilities, brain injury, minimal brain dysfunction, dyslexia, and developmental aphasia" (Nathanson et al., 2007, p. 320).

Chapter 4

1. The suggestions in this section were not tested in randomized trials to assess their independent contributions to the outcome of the interview.

However, many recent studies have demonstrated the value of rapport-building to facilitate communication and motivation, to reduce anxiety and suggestibility, and to increase the accuracy of children's reports. (See Hershkowitz, 2011, for a review.)

Chapter 6

1. In one study, Kulkofsky (2010) did find increased error using verbal cues with very young children when entering the raw number of errors but not the proportion of errors. However, the increase in the raw number of errors was due primarily to the youngest children studied, with a mean age of less than three and a half years, who also demonstrated low vocabulary test scores.

Chapter 7

1. Although other protocols do employ variations of this strategy with young children (e.g., the NICHD Investigative Interview, Event Report Training, and CornerHouse Interview Protocol), we have only tested it with school-age children.

Chapter 8

1. As discussed in detail in Chapter 2, the visual cue cards have been shown to be superior to standard interviews in numerous studies of children three to 12 years of age and children with learning disabilities, low IQ scores, and from disadvantaged backgrounds. The verbal cues, however, produced comparable benefits in one study with typically developing older children. And there is evidence to suggest that somewhat similar verbal category cues improve performance of preschoolers; however, at this time there is no evidence that verbal cues are as effective as the visual cues with pre-interview practice with children under seven, or with children with learning disabilities or children from disadvantaged backgrounds. In addition, only the visual cues, not the verbal cues, have yet been tested with fictitious events to examine false reports.

1. The suggestions in this chapter were not tested in randomized trials to assess their independent contributions to the outcome of the interview. However, they occur after the forensic information-gathering is concluded and some have been tested in mental health treatment outcome studies for their effects on reducing anxiety. Again, readers are encouraged to stay on top of relevant ongoing and future research.

References

American Psychiatric Association. (2000). *Diagnostic and Statistical Manual of Mental Disorders* (4th ed., text rev.). Washington, DC: APA.

Bala, N., Lee, J., & McNamara, E. (2001). Children as witnesses: Understanding their capacities, needs, and experiences. *Journal of Social Distress & the Homeless, 10*, 41–68.

Bauer, P. J. (2007). *Remembering the Times of Our Lives: Memory in Infancy and Beyond. The Developing Mind Series.* Mahwah, NJ: Lawrence Erlbaum Associates Publishers.

Bell, B. E., & Loftus, E. F. (2006). Degree of detail of eyewitness testimony and mock juror judgments. *Journal of Applied Social Psychology, 18*(14), 1171–1192. doi:10.1111/j.1559—1816.19888.tb01200.x

Bidrose, S., & Goodman, G. S. (2000). Testimony and evidence: A scientific case study of memory for child sexual abuse. *Applied Cognitive Psychology, 14*, 197–213.

Boccia, M., & Campos, J. (1989). Maternal emotional signals, social referencing, and infants' reactions to strangers. *New Directions for Child & Adolescent Development, 44*, 25–49. doi:10.1002/cd.23219894404

Bottoms, B. L., Quas, J. A., & Davis, S. L. (2007). The influence of the interviewer-provided social support on children's suggestibility, memory, and disclosures. In M.-E. Pipe, M. E. Lamb, Y. Orbach, & A.-C. Cederborg (Eds.), *Child Sexual Abuse: Disclosure, Delay, and Denial* (pp. 135–153). Mahwah, NJ: Lawrence Erlbaum Associates, Publishers.

Bowen, C. J., & Howie, P. M. (2002). Context and cue cards in young children's testimony: A comparison of brief narrative elaboration and context reinstatement. *Journal of Applied Psychology, 87*, 1077–1085. doi:10.1037//0021-9010.87.6.1077

Brennan, M., & Brennan, R. (1988). *Strange Language: Child Victims Under Cross Examination.* Riverina, Australia: Charles Stuart University.

Brown, D., & Pipe, M.-E. (2003a). Variations on a technique: Enhancing children's recall using Narrative Elaboration training. *Applied Cognitive Psychology, 17*, 377–399.

Brown, D., & Pipe, M.-E. (2003b). Individual differences in children's event memory reports and the Narrative Elaboration technique. *Journal of Applied Psychology, 88,* 195–206.

Bruck, M., Ceci, S. J., Francoeur, E., & Barr, R. (1995). "I hardly cried when I got my shot!" Influencing children's reports about a visit to their pediatrician. *Child Development, 66,* 193–208. doi:10.1111/j.1467-8624.1995.tb00865.x

Bruck, M., Ceci, S. J., & Hembrooke, H. (1998). Reliability and credibility of young children's reports: From research to policy and practice. *American Psychologist, 53,* 136–151.

Bruner, J. S. (1957). On perceptual readiness. *Psychological Review, 64*(2), 123–152. doi:10.1037/h0043805

Camparo, L. B., & Camparo, J. C. (March, 2011). *Developmental differences in children's event memories: Enhancing narrative quality with the Narrative Elaboration and the Verbal Labels procedures.* Presented at the Biennial Meeting for the Society for Research on Child Development, Montreal, Canada.

Camparo, L. B., Wagner, J. T., & Saywitz, K. J. (2001). Interviewing children about real and fictitious events: Revisiting the Narrative Elaboration procedure. *Law & Human Behavior, 25,* 63–80.

Carter, C. A., Bottoms, B. L., & Levine, M. (1996). Linguistic and socioemotional influences on the accuracy of children's reports. *Law & Human Behavior, 20,* 335–358.

Ceci, S. J., Ross, D. F., & Toglia, M. P. (1987). Suggestibility of children's memory: Psycholegal implications. *Journal of Experimental Psychology: General, 116,* 38–49.

Cordón, I. M., Saetermoe, C. L., & Goodman, G. S. (2005). Facilitating children's accurate responses: Conversational rules and interview style. *Applied Cognitive Psychology, 19,* 249–266. doi:10.1002/acp.1090

Cramer, P. (1981). *Development of Defense Mechanisms: Theory, Research, and Assessment.* New York: Springer-Verlag Publishing.

Cronch, L. E., Viljoen, J. L., & Hansen, D. J. (2006). Forensic interviewing in child sexual abuse cases: Current techniques and future directions. *Aggression & Violent Behavior, 11,* 195–207.

Damon, W., & Lerner, R. M. (Eds.). (2006) *Handbook of Child Psychology* (6th ed.). Hoboken, NJ: John Wiley & Sons.

Davies, E., & Seymore, F. W. (1998). Questioning child complainants of sexual abuse: Analysis of criminal court transcripts in New Zealand. *Psychiatry, Psychology & Law, 5,* 47–61.

Davies, G. M., Westcott, H. L., & Horan, N. (2000). The impact of questioning style on the content of investigative interviews with suspected child sexual abuse victims. *Psychology, Crime, & Law, 6*, 81–97.

Deshler, D. D., & Schumaker, J. B. (1993). Strategy mastery by at-risk students: Not a simple matter. *Elementary School Journal, 94*, 153–167.

Dickson, W. (Ed.) (1981). *Children's Oral Communication Skills*. New York: Academic Press.

Dorado, J. S., & Saywitz, K. J. (2001). Interviewing preschoolers from low- and middle-SES communities: A test of the Narrative Elaboration recall improvement technique. *Journal of Clinical Child Psychology, 30*, 568–580.

Elischberger, H. B., & Roebers, C. M. (2001). Improving young children's free narratives about an observed event: The effects of nonspecific verbal prompts. *International Journal of Behavioral Development, 25*(2), 160–166.

Endres, J., Poggenpohl, C., & Erben, C. (1999). Repetitions, warnings and video: Cognitive and motivational components in preschool children's suggestibility. *Legal & Criminological Psychology, 4*, 129–146.

Evans, A. D., Lee, K., & Lyon, T. D. (2009). Complex questions asked by defense lawyers but not prosecutors predicts convictions in child abuse trials. *Law & Human Behavior, 33*, 258–264.

Flavell, J. H. (1981). Cognitive monitoring. In W. P. Dickson (Ed.), *Children's Oral Communication Skills* (pp. 35–60). New York: Academic Press.

Flavell, J. H. (1985). *Cognitive Development* (rev. ed). Englewood Cliffs, NJ: Prentice-Hall.

Flavell, J. H., Botkin, P. T., Fry, C. L., Wright, J. W., & Jarvis, P. E.(1968*). The Development of Role Taking and Communication Skills in Children*. New York: Wiley.

Flavell, J. H., & Miller, P. H. (1998). Social cognition. In W. Damon (Ed.), *Handbook of Child Psychology: Volume 2: Cognition, Perception, and Language* (pp. 851–898). Hoboken, NJ: John Wiley & Sons.

Flin, R. H., Stevenson, Y., & Davies, G. M. (1989). Children's knowledge of court proceedings. *British Journal of Psychology, 80*, 285–297.

Garven, S., Wood, J. M., & Malpass, R. S. (2000). Allegations of wrongdoing: The effects of reinforcement on children's mundane and fantastic claims. *Journal of Applied Psychology, 85*, 38–49.

Geddie, L. F., Beer, J., Bartosik, S., & Wuensch, K. L. (2001). The relationship between interview characteristics and accuracy of recall in young children: Do individual differences matter? *Child Maltreatment, 6*(1), 59–68.

Geddie, L., Fradin, S., & Beer, J. (2000). Child characteristics which impact accuracy of recall and suggestibility in preschoolers: Is age the best predictor? *Child Abuse & Neglect, 24*, 223–235.

Gee, S., Gregory, M., & Pipe, M.-E. (1999). "What colour is your pet dinosaur?" The impact of pre-interview training and question type on children's answers. *Legal & Criminological Psychology, 4*(1), 111–128.

Goodman, G. S., & Melinder, A. (2007). Child witness research and forensic interviews in young children: A review. *Legal & Criminological Psychology, 12*, 1–19.

Goodman, G. S., Sharma, A., Thomas, S. F., & Considine, M. G. (1995). Mother knows best: Effects of relationship status and interviewer bias on children's memory. *Journal of Experimental Child Psychology, 60*, 195–228.

Goodman, G. S., Tobey, A. E., Batterman-Faunce, J. M., Orcutt, H., Thomas, S., Shapiro, C., et al. (1998). Face-to-face confrontation: Effects of closed-circuit technology on children's eyewitness testimony and jurors' decisions. *Law & Human Behavior, 22*, 165–203.

Gopnik, A. (2009). *The Philosophical Baby*. New York: Farrar, Straus & Giroux.

Harari, H., & McDavid, J. W. (1969). Situational influences on moral justice: A study of "finking." *Journal of Personality & Social Psychology, 11*, 240–244.

Hershkowitz, I. (2009). Socioemotional factors in child abuse investigations. *Child Maltreatment, 12*(2), 172–181.

Hershkowitz, I. (2011). Rapport building in investigative interviews of children. In M. E. Lamb, D. J. LaRooy, L. C. Malloy, & C. Katz (Eds.), *Children's Testimony: A Handbook of Psychological Research and Forensic Practice* (pp. 109–128). Malden, MA: Wiley-Blackwell.

Hershkowitz, I., Orbach, Y., Lamb, M. E., Sternberg, K. J., & Horowitz, D. (2006). Dynamics of forensic interviews with suspected abuse victims who do not disclose abuse. *Child Abuse & Neglect, 30*, 753–769.

Holtz, B. A., & Lehman, E. B. (1995). Development of children's knowledge and use of strategies for self-control in a resistance-to-distraction task. *Merrill-Palmer Quarterly: Journal of Developmental Psychology, 41*, 361–380.

Hughes, M., & Grieve, R. (1980). On asking children bizarre questions. *First Language, 1*, 149–160.

Idaho v. Wright, 110 S.Ct. 3139 (1990).

Ingram, D. (1976). Phonological analysis of a child. *Glossa, 10*, 3–27.

Kannass, K. N., Colombo, J., & Wyss, N. (2010). Now, pay attention? The effects of instruction on children's attention. *Journal of Cognition & Development, 11*(4), 509–532.

Kintsch, W., & Van Dijk, T. A. (1978). Toward a model of text comprehension and production. *Psychological Review, 85*, 363–394.

Kobasigawa, A. (1977). Retrieval strategies in the development of memory. In R. V. Kail, Jr., & J. W. Hagen (Eds.), *Perspectives on the Development of Memory and Cognition (pp. 177–201)*. Hillsdale, NJ: Lawrence Erlbaum Associates Publishers.

Krackow, E. (2010). Narratives distinguish experienced from imagined childhood events. *American Journal of Psychology, 123*(1), 71–80.

Krackow, E., & Lynn, S. (2009). Event report training: An examination of the efficacy of a new intervention to improve children's eyewitness reports. *Applied Cognitive Psychology*. doi:10.1002/acp.1594

Kulkofsky, S. (2010). The effects of verbal labels and vocabulary skill on memory and suggestibility. *Journal of Applied Developmental Psychology, 31*, 460–466. doi:10.10.16/j.app.dev.2010.09.002

Kulkofsky, S., & Klemfuss, J. Z. (2008). What the stories children tell can tell about their memory: Narrative skill and young children's suggestibility. *Developmental Psychology, 44*, 1442–1456. doi:10.1037/a0012849

Kulkofsky, S., Wang, Q., & Ceci, S. J. (2008). Do better stories make better memories? Narrative quality and memory accuracy in preschool children. *Applied Cognitive Psychology, 22*, 21–38. doi:10.1002/acp.1326

Lamb, M. E., & Brown, D. A. (2006). Conversational apprentices: Helping children become competent informants about their own experiences. *British Journal of Developmental Psychology, 24*, 215–234.

Lamb, M. E., LaRooy, D. J., Malloy, L. C., & Katz, C. (2011). *Children's Testimony: A Handbook of Psychological Research and Forensic Practice*. Malden, MA: Wiley-Blackwell.

Lamb, M. E., Orbach, Y., Hershkowitz, I., Esplin, P., & Horowitz, D. (2007). Structured forensic interview protocols improve the quality and informativeness of investigative interviews with children: A review of research using the NICHD Investigative Interview Protocol. *International Journal of Child Abuse and Neglect, 31*(11–12), 1201–1231.

Lamb, M. E., Sternberg, K. J., Orbach, Y., Esplin, P. W., Stewart, H., & Mitchell, S. (2003). Age differences in young children's responses to open-ended invitations in the course of forensic interviews. *Journal of Consulting & Clinical Psychology, 71*, 926–934.

Lanktree, C., Briere, J., & Zaidi, L. (1991). Incidence and impact of sexual abuse in a child outpatient sample: The role of direct inquiry. *Child Abuse & Neglect, 15*, 447–453.

Larsson, A. S., & Lamb, M. E. (2009). Making the most of information-gathering interviews with children. *Infant & Child Development, 18*, 1–16. doi:10.1002/ICD.573

Leander, L., Christianson, S. A., & Granhag, P. A. (2007). A sexual abuse case study: Children's memories and report. *Psychiatry, Psychology, & Law, 14*, 120–129.

Leichtman, M. D., & Ceci, S. J. (1995). The effects of stereotypes and suggestions on preschoolers' reports. *Developmental Psychology, 31*, 568–578.

Lepore, S. J., & Sesco, B. (1994). Distorting children's reports and interpretations of events through suggestion. *Journal of Applied Psychology, 79*, 108–120.

Lyon, T. D. (2007). False denials: Overcoming methodological biases in abuse disclosure research. In M.-E. Pipe, M. E. Lamb, Y. Orbach, & A.-C. Cederborg (Eds.), *Child Sexual Abuse: Disclosure, Delay, and Denial* (pp. 41–62). Mahwah, NJ: Lawrence Erlbaum Associates, Publishers.

Lyon, T. D., Ahern, E. C., Malloy, L. C., & Quas, J. A. (2010). Children's reasoning about disclosing adult transgressions: Effects of maltreatment, child age, and adult identity. *Child Development, 81*, 1714–1728.

Lyon, T. D., Malloy, L. C., Quas, J. A., & Talwar, V. (2008). Coaching, truth induction, and young maltreated children's false allegations and false denials. *Child Development, 79*, 914–929.

Mandler, J. M., & Johnson, N. S. (1977). Remembrance of things parsed: Story structure and recall. *Cognitive Psychology, 9*, 111–151.

Markman, E. M. (1981). Comprehension monitoring. In W. P. Dickson (Ed.), *Children's Oral and Communication Skills* (pp. 61–84). New York: Academic Press.

McCauley, M. R., & Fisher R. P. (1995). Facilitating children's eyewitness recall with the revised cognitive interview. *Journal of Applied Psychology, 80*, 510–516.

Memon, A., & Vartoukian, R. (1996). The effects of repeated questioning on young children's eyewitness testimony. *British Journal of Psychology, 87*(3), 403–415.

Memon, A., Wark, L., Bull, R., & Koehnken, G. (1997). Isolating the effects of the cognitive interview techniques. *British Journal of Psychology, 88*(2), 179–197.

Milne, R., & Bull, R. (2003). Does the cognitive interview help children to resist the effects of suggestive questioning. *Legal and Criminological Psychology, 8*, 1, 21–38.

Moore, C., & Furrow, D. (1991). The development of the language of belief. In D. Frye & C. Moore (Eds.), *Children's Theories of Mind: Mental States and Social Understanding* (pp. 173–194). Hillsdale, NJ: Lawrence Erlbaum Associates.

Moston, S. (1987). The suggestibility of children in interview studies. *First Language, 7,* 67–78.

Nathanson, R., Crank, J. N., Saywitz, K. J., & Ruegg, E. (2007). Enhancing the oral narratives of children with learning disabilities. *Reading & Writing Quarterly, 23,* 315–331.

Nathanson, R., & Saywitz, K. J. (2003). The effects of the courtroom context on children's memory and anxiety. *Journal of Psychiatry & Law, 31,* 67–98.

Nelson, K. (1986). *Event Knowledge: Structure and Function in Development.* Hillsdale, NJ: Lawrence Erlbaum.

Nelson, K., & Fivush, R. (2004). The emergence of autobiographical memory: A social cultural developmental theory. *Psychological Review, 111,* 486–511.

Normand, K. E., Camparo, L. B., & Almeria, H. (April, 2012). *Descriptive quality of children's narratives about real and fictitious events: A comparison of three interview protocols.* Presented at the Convention for the Western Psychological Association, San Francisco, CA.

Ornstein, P. A., Naus, M. J., & Liberty, C. (1975). Rehearsal and organizational processes in children's memory. *Child Development, 46,* 818–830.

Owens, R. E. (2011). *Language Development: An Introduction* (8th ed.). Boston, MA: Allyn & Bacon.

Perona, A. R., Bottoms, B. L., & Sorenson, E. (2006). Research-based guidelines for child forensic interviews. *Journal of Aggression, Maltreatment, & Trauma, 12,* 81–130.

Perry, N. W., McAuliff, B. D., Tam, P., Claycomb, L., Dostal, C., & Flanagan, C. (1995). When lawyers question children: Is justice served? *Law & Human Behavior, 19,* 609–629.

Peters, W. W., & Nunez, N. (1999). Complex language and comprehension monitoring: Teaching child witnesses to recognize linguistic confusion. *Journal of Applied Psychology, 84,* 661–669.

Peterson, C. (1990). The who, when, where of early narratives. *Journal of Child Language, 17*(2), 433–455.

Peterson, C., & Bell, M. (1996). Children's memory of traumatic injury. *Child Development, 67,* 3045–3070.

Peterson, C., & Warren, L. K. (2009). Injuries, emergency rooms, and children's memory: Factors contributing to individual differences. In J. A. Quas & R. Fivush (Eds.), *Emotion and Memory in Development: Biological, Cognitive, and Social Considerations* (pp. 60–85). New York: Oxford University Press.

Peterson, C., Warren, K. L., & Hayes, A. H. (2013). Revisiting the Narrative Elaboration training: An ecologically relevant event. *Journal of Cognition & Development, 14*(1), 154–174. doi:10.1080/15248372.2011.638688

Peterson, C., & Whalen, N. (2001). Five years later: Children's memory for medical emergencies. *Applied Cognitive Psychology, 15*(7), S7–S24.

Piaget, J. (1926). *The Language and Thought of the Child.* New York: Harcourt, Brace & Co.

Piaget, J. (1930). *The Child's Conception of Physical Causality.* London: Kegan Paul. (Republished: Totowa, NJ: Littlefield, Adams, 1967).

Pipe, M. E., Lamb, M. E., Orbach, Y., & Esplin, P. W. (2004). Recent research on children's testimony about experienced and witnessed events. *Developmental Review, 24,* 440–468.

Plotnikoff, J., & Woolfson, R. (2009). *Measuring Up? Evaluating Implementation of Government Commitments to Young Witnesses in Criminal Proceedings.* London: National Society for the Prevention of Cruelty to Children (NSPCC).

Poole, D. A., & Lindsay, D. S. (1995). Interviewing preschoolers: Effects of nonsuggestive techniques, parental coaching, and leading questions on reports of nonexperienced events. *Journal of Experimental Child Psychology, 60,* 129–154.

Pressley, M., & Levin, J. R. (1977). Task parameters affecting the efficacy of a visual imagery learning strategy for younger and older children. *Journal of Experimental Child Psychology, 24,* 53–59.

Quas. J. A., Malloy, L. C., Melinder, A., Goodman, G. S., D'Mello, M., & Schaaf, J. (2007). Developmental differences in the effects of repeated interviews and interviewer bias on young children's event memory and false reports. *Developmental Psychology, 43,* 823–837.

Quas, J. A., & Sumaroka, M. (2011). Consequences of legal involvement on child victims of maltreatment. In M. E. Lamb, D. J. La Rooy, L. C. Malloy, & C. Katz (Eds.), *Children's Testimony: A Handbook of Psychological Research and Forensic Practice* (pp. 323–350). Malden, MA: Wiley-Blackwell.

Quas, J. A., Wallin, A. R., Horowitz, B., Davis, E., & Lyon, T. D. (2009). Maltreated children's understanding of and emotional reactions to dependency court involvement. *Behavioral Sciences & the Law, 27,* 97–117.

Roberts, K. P., Lamb, M. E., & Sternberg, K. J. (2004). The effects of rapport-building style on children's reports of a staged event. *Applied Cognitive Psychology, 18,* 189–202.

Robinson, E. J., & Robinson, W. P. (1978). Explanations of communication failure and ability to give bad messages. *British Journal of Social & Clinical Psychology, 17,* 219–225.

Salatas, H., & Flavell, J. H. (1976). Retrieval of recently learned information: Development of strategies and control skills. *Child Development, 47,* 941–948.

Sas, L, Austin, G., Wolfe, D., & Hurley, P. (1991). *Reducing the System-Induced Trauma for Child Sexual Abuse Victims Through Court Preparation, Assessment and Follow-up* (Final Report for Project #4555-1-125). Canada: Health and Welfare, Canada, National Welfare Grants Division.

Sas, L., Hurley, P., Hatch, A., Malla, S., & Dick, T. (1993). *Three Years After the Verdict: A Longitudinal Study of the Social and Psychological Adjustment of Child Witnesses Referred to the Child Witness Project.* Ottawa, Canada: Health and Welfare Canada.

Saywitz, K. J. (1989). Children's conception of the legal system: Court is a place to play basketball. In S. Ceci, D. Ross, & M. Toglia (Eds.), *Perspectives on Children's Testimony* (pp. 131–157). New York: Springer-Verlag Publishing.

Saywitz, K. J., & Camparo, L. B. (2009). Contemporary child forensic interviewing: Evolving consensus and innovation over 25 years. In B. L. Bottoms, C. J. Najdowski, & G. S. Goodman (Eds.), *Children as Victims, Witnesses, and Offenders* (pp. 102–127). New York: The Guilford Press.

Saywitz, K. J., Esplin, P., & Romanoff, S. (2007). A holistic approach to interviewing and treating children in the legal system. In M.-E. Pipe, M. E. Lamb, Y. Orbach, & A.-C. Cederborg (Eds.), *Child Sexual Abuse: Disclosure, Delay, and Denial* (pp. 219–250). Mahwah, NJ: Lawrence Erlbaum Associates, Publishers.

Saywitz, K. J., Geiselman, R. E., & Bornstein, G. K. (1992). Effects of cognitive interviewing and practice on children's recall performance. *Journal of Applied Psychology, 77,* 744–756.

Saywitz, K., Jaenicke, C., & Camparo, L. (1990). Children's knowledge of legal terminology. *Law & Human Behavior, 14,* 523–535.

Saywitz, K. J., Lyon, T. D., & Goodman, G. S. (2011). Interviewing children. In J. E. B. Meyers (Ed.), *The APSAC Handbook on Child Maltreatment* (3rd ed.; pp 337–360). Los Angeles: Sage Publications.

Saywitz, K. J., & Moan-Hardie, S. (1994). Reducing the potential for distortion of childhood memories. *Consciousness & Cognition, 3,* 408–425.

Saywitz, K. J., & Nathanson, R. (1993a). Children's testimony and their perceptions of stress in and out of the courtroom. *Child Abuse & Neglect, 17,* 613–622.

Saywitz, K. J., & Nathanson, R. (1993b). Court education and stress reduction curriculum. In K. J. Saywitz, R. Nathanson, L. Snyder, & V. Lamphear (Eds.), *Preparing Children for the Investigative and Judicial Process: Improving Communication, Memory and Emotional Resiliency* (Final Report to the National Center on Child Abuse and Neglect, Grant No. 90-CA-1179). Los Angeles: University of California.

Saywitz, K. J., Nathanson, R., Snyder, L., & Lamphear, V. (1993). *Preparing Children for the Investigative and Judicial Process: Improving Communication, Memory and Emotional Resiliency* (Final Report to the National Center on Child Abuse and Neglect, Grant No. 90-CA-1179). Los Angeles: University of California.

Saywitz, K. J., & Snyder, L. (1996). Narrative Elaboration: Test of a new procedure for interviewing children. *Journal of Consulting & Clinical Psychology, 64*, 1347–1357.

Saywitz, K. J., Snyder, L., & Lamphear, V. (1996). Helping children tell what happened: A follow-up study of the Narrative Elaboration procedure. *Child Maltreatment, 1*, 200–212.

Saywitz, K. J., Snyder, L., & Nathanson, R. (1999). Facilitating the communicative competence of the child witness. *Applied Developmental Science 3*, 58–68.

Saywitz, K. J., & Wilkinson, L. (1982). Age-related differences in metalinguistic awareness. In S. Kuczaj (Ed.), *Language Development: Vol. 2. Language, Thought and Culture* (pp. 229–250). Hillsdale, NJ: Erlbaum.

Schneider, W., & Pressley, M. (1989). *Memory Development Between Two and Twenty. Springer Series on Cognitive Development* New York: Springer-Verlag Publishing.

Scott, C. M., & Windsor, J. (2000). General language performance measures in spoken and written narrative and expository discourse of school-age children with language learning disabilities. *Journal of Speech, Language, & Hearing Research, 43*, 324–339.

Shantz, C. (1975). *The Development of Social Cognition*. Chicago, IL: University of Chicago Press.

Stein, N. L., & Glenn, C. G. (1978). An analysis of story comprehension in elementary school children. In R. O. Freedle (Ed.), *Multidisciplinary Perspectives in Discourse Comprehension*. Hillsdale, NJ: Ablex.

Steinmetz, S. K. (1971). Occupation and physical punishment: A response to Straus. *Journal of Marriage & the Family, 33*, 664–666.

Sternberg, K. J., Lamb, M. E., Hershkowitz, I., Esplin, P. W., Redlich, A., & Sunshine, N. (1996). The relation between investigative utterance types and the informativeness of child witnesses. *Journal of Applied Developmental Psychology, 17*, 439–451.

Sternberg, K. J., Lamb, M. E., Hershkowitz, I., Yudilevitch, L., Orbach, Y., Esplin, P. W., et al. (1997). Effects of introductory style on children's abilities to describe experiences of sexual abuse. *Child Abuse & Neglect, 21*, 1133–1146.

Straus, M. A., Gelles, R. J., & Steinmetz, S. K. (1980). *Behind Closed Doors: Violence in the American Family.* Garden City, NY: Anchor Books.

Taylor, M., Cartwright, B. S., & Bowden, T. (1991). Perspective taking and theory of mind: Do children predict interpretive diversity as a function of differences in observers' knowledge? *Child Development, 62*, 1334–1351. doi:10.1111/j.1467-8624.1991.tb01609.x

Toglia, M. P., Ross, D. F., Ceci, S. J., & Hembrooke, H. (1992). The suggestibility of children's memory: A social psychological and cognitive interpretation. In M. L. Howe, C. J. Brainerd, & V. R. Reyna (Eds.), *Development of Long-Term Retention.* New York: Springer-Verlag.

Walker, N. E., Lunning, S., & Eilts, J. L. (1996). Do children respond accurately to forced choice questions? Yes or no. *Recollections of Trauma: Scientific Research and Clinical Practice.* NATO Advanced Study Institute on Recollections of Trauma: Scientific and Clinical Practice. Talmont Saint Hilaire, France.

Wandrey, L., Lyon, T. D., Quas, J. A., & Friedman, W. J. (2011). Maltreated children's ability to estimate temporal location and numerosity of placement changes and court visits. *Psychology, Public Policy & the Law, 18*(1), 79–104.

Warren, A., Hulse-Trotter, K., & Tubbs, E. (1991). Inducing resistance to suggestibility in children. *Law & Human Behavior, 15*(3), 273–285.

Warren-Leubecker, A., Tate, C., Hinton, I., & Ozbek, N. (1989). What do children know about the legal system and when do they know it? In S. J. Ceci, D. F. Ross, & M. P. Toglia (Eds.), *Perspectives on Children's Testimony* (pp. 131–157). New York: Springer-Verlag.

Waterman, A. H., Blades, M., & Spencer, C. (2001). Interviewing children and adults: The effect of question format on the tendency to speculate. *Applied Cognitive Psychology, 15*, 521–531.

White, T. L., Leichtman, M. D., & Ceci, S. J. (1997). The good, the bad, and the ugly: Accuracy, inaccuracy, and elaboration in preschoolers' reports about past events. *Applied Cognitive Psychology, 11*, S37–S54.

Wilson, K. (2007). Forensic interviewing in New Zealand. In M.-E. Pipe, M. E. Lamb, Y. Orbach, & A.-C. Cederborg (Eds.), *Child Sexual Abuse: Disclosure, Delay, and Denial* (pp. 265–280). Mahwah, NJ: Lawrence Erlbaum Associates, Publishers.

About the Authors

Karen Saywitz, PhD, is a professor in the Department of Psychiatry and Biobehavioral Sciences at the University of California, Los Angeles School of Medicine. For 20 years she has trained students in medicine, psychology, social work, nursing, and law on the development of children and adolescents, and has directed programs providing mental health services to children and families in the public sector. She has authored numerous articles regarding the capabilities, limitations, and needs of children in the legal system, including a bench-book for California judges. Her co-authored papers have been cited by the U.S. Supreme Court and numerous U.S. appellate courts. In her research on interviewing children and preparing them for court, Dr. Saywitz develops and tests innovative interventions to enhance children's memory performance, communicative competence, emotional resilience, and resistance to suggestion. She is a past president of the American Psychological Association's Division of Child, Youth and Family Services. She has been the recipient of awards for her pioneering research, outstanding teaching, and distinguished clinical service, including the Nicholas Hobbs Award for Child Advocacy from the APA Society for Child and Family Policy and Practice, and the Research Career Achievement Award from the American Professional Society on the Abuse of Children.

Lorinda B. Camparo, PhD, received her doctorate in developmental psychology from the University of California–Los Angeles in 1994. She is currently a professor in the Psychology Department at Whittier College, where she has taught and conducted research on child forensic interviewing with undergraduate students since 1997. Dr. Camparo has co-authored numerous articles and book chapters, and she and her students have presented research nationally and internationally. Beyond the Whittier community, Dr. Camparo has been an active member of the Executive Committee for the Society for Child and Family Policy and Practice (APA Division 37) for the past 15 years, serving as program chair for the millennium convention, editor of *The Advocate*, and member-at-large for Communication and Technology. Dr. Camparo has also conducted workshops on interviewing children for lawyers, judges, police officers, and social workers, and has served as an expert witness on cases involving children alleging sexual abuse. As a child development expert, Dr. Camparo has been interviewed for the television news shows *World News Tonight* and *Good Morning America*.